THE REAL QUEEN CHARLOTTE

To Helen, for all those worlds.

THE REAL QUEEN CHARLOTTE

INSIDE THE REAL BRIDGERTON COURT

CATHERINE CURZON

WHITE OWL

AN IMPRINT OF PEN & SWORD BOOKS LTD.
YORKSHIRE – PHILADELPHIA

First published in Great Britain in 2022 by
PEN AND SWORD WHITE OWL
An imprint of
Pen & Sword Books Ltd
Yorkshire - Philadelphia

ISBN 978 1 39909 701 7

Typeset in Times New Roman 12/16 by SJmagic DESIGN SERVICES, India.
Printed and bound in the UK by CPI Group (UK) Ltd.

Pen & Sword Books Ltd incorporates the Imprints of Pen & Sword Books
Archaeology, Atlas, Aviation, Battleground, Discovery, Family History,
History, Maritime, Military, Naval, Politics, Railways, Select, Transport, True
Crime, Fiction, Frontline Books, Leo Cooper, Praetorian Press, Seaforth
Publishing, Wharncliffe and White Owl.

For a complete list of Pen & Sword titles please contact
PEN & SWORD BOOKS LIMITED
47 Church Street, Barnsley, South Yorkshire, S70 2AS, England
E-mail: enquiries@pen-and-sword.co.uk
Website: www.pen-and-sword.co.uk

Or

PEN AND SWORD BOOKS
1950 Lawrence Rd, Havertown, PA 19083, USA
E-mail: Uspen-and-sword@casematepublishers.com
Website: www.penandswordbooks.com

Contents

Acknowledgements

It's tea and cake all round at Pen and Sword, with the finest chips for Jon. An extra special thanks to Cecily, for whipping Queen Charlotte into shape.

Now for the usual suspects… A gin-soaked *rococo 'n' roll* to Rob and Kathy, who have been the very, very best.

Pippa, Nelly, and the Rakish Colonial – keep watching the skies!

The Royal Family

In a few generations there will be no joke in saying
Their Highnesses the Mob.[1]

In their first twenty-two years of marriage, George III and Charlotte of Mecklenburg-Strelitz became parents to fifteen children. Their names are below, with the names of their spouses – legal or otherwise – in italics. Rumoured marriages are not included.

George IV (12 August 1762–26 June 1830)
  Maria Fitzherbert (m.1785; not legally recognised)
  Princess Caroline of Brunswick-Wolfenbüttel (m.1795; separated)

Prince Frederick, Duke of York and Albany (16 August 1763–5 January 1827)
  Princess Frederica of Prussia (m.1791; separated)

William IV (21 August 1765–20 June 1837)
  Princess Adelaide of Saxe-Meiningen (m.1818)

Charlotte, Princess Royal (29 September 1766–6 October 1828)
  King Frederick of Württemberg (m.1797)
Prince Edward, Duke of Kent and Strathearn (2 November 1767–23 January 1820)
  Princess Victoria of Saxe-Coburg-Saalfeld (m.1818)

Princess Augusta Sophia (8 November 1768–22 September 1840)

Princess Elizabeth (22 May 1770–10 January 1840)
  Frederick, Landgrave of Hesse-Homburg (m.1818)

Ernest Augustus, King of Hanover (5 June 1771–18 November 1851)
  Princess Frederica of Mecklenburg-Strelitz (m.1815)

Prince Augustus Frederick, Duke of Sussex (27 January 1773–21 April 1843)
  Lady Augusta Murray (m.1793; annulled)
  Lady Cecilia Buggin (m.1831)

Prince Adolphus, Duke of Cambridge (24 February 1774–8 July 1850)
  Princess Augusta of Hesse-Kassel (m.1818)

Princess Mary, Duchess of Gloucester and Edinburgh (25 April 1776–30 April 1857)
  Prince William Frederick, Duke of Gloucester and Edinburgh (m.1816)

Princess Sophia (3 November 1777–27 May 1848)

Prince Octavius (23 February 1779–3 May 1783)

Prince Alfred (22 September 1780–20 August 1782)

Princess Amelia (7 August 1783–2 November 1810)

Introduction

> [Charlotte] is not tall, nor a beauty; pale, and very thin; but looks sensible, and is genteel. Her hair is darkish and fine; her forehead low, her nose very well, except the nostrils spreading too wide; her mouth has the same fault, but her teeth are good. She talks a good deal and French tolerably; possesses herself, is frank, but with great respect to the King.[1]

Charlotte of Mecklenburg-Strelitz was not born to greatness. She was quiet, unassuming, and raised in a little corner of Europe from which it seemed unlikely that any queen would emerge. Yet when it came to royal marriages, a mostly forgotten little corner might turn out to be just what was needed.

When George II died in 1760, his son and heir, Frederick, was already dead. The crown passed to Fred's 22-year-old son, the timid, unassuming George III. He would reign for nearly sixty years. At his side through thick and thin was Queen Charlotte, the girl from Mecklenburg-Strelitz.

What made Charlotte so remarkable was the very fact that she wasn't remarkable at all. Unpolitical, unambitious, and aspiring only to a happy home, she was a gift to the politicians who hoped to keep the young George III in check. At first, Charlotte got her wish. Though she had never met her groom before the wedding day, their marriage was loving, faithful, and mundane in its domesticity. There was not a trace of the tumultuous roller-coaster of infidelity, divorce, and murder that had tainted the marriage of George I, nor of the politically ambitious queen and procession of mistresses who had held sway at the court of George II. George III was at pains to prove to his subjects that he was not so different to them. He strove to demonstrate his Englishness, downplayed his German ancestry, and shared his bride's love of home and hearth. It should have been a match made in heaven, but fate had other things in store.

Queen Charlotte and King George III were married for nearly sixty years. Their union was blighted by the king's ill health and, as his wife became more keeper than companion, she mourned for the man she had known and loved. That unassuming, optimistic girl was dragged into a life that she had little anticipated, where she fled in terror from her husband's rages, locked the bedroom door against him at night, and sought solace in her unhappy, cosseted daughters. As the royal family erupted into all-out war between the queen and the eldest son who would be Regent, what had once been a happy home became a battleground.

Yet Queen Charlotte was more than the stand-by-your-man wife at the side of an ailing husband or the gossip-hungry matriarch of the *Bridgerton* court. She lived through tumultuous times, and her journey from that little corner of Europe to queen of one of the grandest courts in the world is as fascinating now as it ever was. Poised, devoted, difficult, and with a temper that would send her children scattering, this is the story of the real Queen Charlotte.

'Think of the Crown of England and a handsome young King dropping from the clouds into Strelitz! The crowds, the multitudes, the millions, that are to stare at her; the swarms to kiss her hand, the pomp of the Coronation. She need be but seventeen to bear it!'

Horace Walpole, 4th Earl of Orford, to Horace
Mann, 17 August 1761

'The King I think remarkably well; the Queen as usual, sometimes *sweet* & sometimes *sour*.'

Princess Amelia to the
Prince of Wales, October 1806

Act One

Princess

No lack of Daughters, nor of Sons by-and-by; eight years hence came the little Charlotte, subsequently Mother of England, much to her and our astonishment.[1]

Mother of England

The childhoods of royal daughters do not always make for a happy story. In the Hanoverian family tree alone, one can find children ripped from the arms of their mothers, never to be reunited, sons thrashed for stepping out of line, and daughters locked away, cosseted in perpetual girlhood. For Sophie Charlotte of Mecklenburg-Strelitz, however, things were rather different.

If Great Britain was a superpower, Mecklenburg was anything but. Just 120 miles long and 30 wide, it petered out into the Baltic Sea in the north and its borders were crowded by Brandenburg, Luneburg, and Holstein. Mecklenburg had once been a powerful home to the Vandals, but as their dominance decreased, they were pushed further and further back until it was their only stronghold. Here they reinforced their kingdom until they fell beneath the forces of Henry the Lion, Duke of Saxony. Duke Henry brought Christianity to the conquered people of Mecklenburg, and hot on his heels followed an influx of new arrivals from Germany and the Low Countries. Once the stronghold of warlords, Mecklenburg was changing beyond recognition.

Over centuries, the German territories were reshaped and carved up, used as bargaining chips and dowries in a never-ending European powerplay. In 1701, the Treaty of Hamburg established the Duchy of Mecklenburg-Strelitz, a far from important state of the immensely powerful Holy Roman Empire. Mecklenburg was simply one of dozens of duchies that the Empire hoovered up to secure its power, but it proved extraordinarily good at producing queens.[2]

Sophie Charlotte's father, Duke Charles Louis Frederick of Mecklenburg, was born in Strelitz in 1708. He was the younger son of Adolphus Frederick II, the reigning Duke of Mecklenburg-Strelitz, and the half-brother of *another* Adolphus Frederick, who eventually succeeded their father to rule over the duchy in 1708. Just three months old when his father died, young Charles Louis inherited the commandries of Mirow and Nemerow. A commandery was the smallest territory anyone could administer and even in Mecklenburg, where large was relative, it paled in comparison to the lands controlled by Adolphus Frederick III. Charles didn't mind, though. It was all a matter of birthright, after all.

The infant Charles Louis was taken by his bereaved mother to the family estate at Mirow, where he was raised. Mirow was a rather sorry place, by far the lesser of the Mecklenburg territories, just as the Strelitz branch of the House was lesser to the others, and Charles Louis' education was rather wanting too. Still, he lived the life of a noble young gentleman, eventually leaving Mirow for Pomerania and a programme of study at the University of Greifswald. The 18-year-old Charles Louis also undertook the requisite Grand Tour of Europe, a coming-of-age rite of passage for highborn young men. With little calling him home, he entered the military in the service of the Holy Roman Empire, serving to little fanfare before he finally returned to Mirow.

Upon his return to his childhood home, Charles Louis was ready to settle down. He took as his wife Princess Elisabeth Albertine of

Saxe-Hildburghausen, and though theirs was a marriage of minor dynastic importance for two minor dynastic families, it was one founded on love. Their union seemed to signal a new beginning in Mirow and soon the little court was beginning to flourish. Though far from wealthy, the young couple's presence ignited a spark that revitalised all of the land. Yet as his territories prospered and Charles Louis threw himself into their improvement, his health began to fail. He already suffered from recurrent bouts of pulmonary illness and, as the years passed, they grew ever more serious.

Elisabeth Albertine was the daughter of Ernest Frederick I, Duke of Saxe-Hildburghausen, and Countess Sophia Albertine of Erbach-Erbach. Like Charles Louis in Mirow, their life was hardly illustrious. Ernest Frederick was a soldier who had dreamed of recreating the splendid Bourbon court on his home turf, but instead he managed to wring the treasury dry. With his lands on the brink of revolt, Ernest Frederick tried to raise funds by selling his wife's dowry, the county of Cuylenburg. Saxe-Meiningen purchased the county, not realising that Sophia Albertine hadn't consented to the sale, which she was legally required to do. Once the truth got out, Saxe-Meiningen and Saxe-Hildburghausen entered into a ruinous territorial war that devastated the land. It wasn't until Ernest Frederick's death that the financial situation in Saxe-Hildburghausen came under control. His widow, it turned out, was more of a ruler than he had ever been.

It was from this unsettled court that Elisabeth Albertine came to Mirow. Perhaps unsurprisingly, given the example of her mother, when Elisabeth Albertine was called upon to prove her mettle many years after her marriage,[3] she proved herself more than capable. She and Charles Louis eventually had ten children, four of whom died in infancy. Of the six who survived to adulthood, Sophie Charlotte was the longest-lived.

The Seat of Every Social Virtue

Sophie Charlotte of Mecklenburg-Strelitz was born on 19 May 1744 at the Unteres Schloss in Mirow. She was the eighth child and fifth daughter – though three died in infancy – of the Duke and Duchess, who had passed nine years of happily married life. There was nothing to suggest that this latest arrival might become a queen, and nothing to suggest that anyone as lofty as the King of Great Britain might ever even know that she existed.

When it came to raising their children, Charles Louis and Elisabeth Albertine didn't stand on ceremony. The couple personally oversaw their education and under the watchful eye of Reverend Gottlob Burchard Gentmer, a Lutheran minister, Sophie Charlotte and her older sister, Christiane, were subject to a regime with two things at its heart: faith and family.

Gentmer was particularly passionate about the sciences and the little siblings soon shared their tutor's excitement about everything from minerology to botany, which was Sophie Charlotte's particular passion throughout her life. Though Gentmer couldn't teach the girls English because he didn't speak it himself, Sophie Charlotte did study French, the language of the courts of Europe, and she proved herself to be a placid and industrious student who was keen to learn. The girls and their brothers studied European literature, history, geography, and a great many classes of arts and sciences. Though botany was always one of Sophie Charlotte's keenest interests, Gentmer also shared with her his enthusiasm for mineralogy. During his research, he had assembled an impressive collection of fossils, which was considered to be one of the best in Europe, and Sophie Charlotte was fascinated by it. In the years to come, Sophie Charlotte's interest in mineralogy never waned and, when queen, she became the patron of Jean André Deluc, the Swiss geologist and meteorologist.[4]

Perhaps we can best see the difference in the fate that awaited the brothers and sisters when we consider that, whilst her brother was appointed rector of the University of Greifswald at the age of just 15 and delivered a self-composed Latin oration on the occasion, Sophie Charlotte was being trained in household management. Not for her the lofty ivory towers of higher education. Instead, she was already well on the way to becoming the very picture of a philanthropic gentlewoman. She excelled in botany, needlework, and music and undertook regular trips to the poor of the duchy, dispensing charity and taking a very real interest in the wellbeing of those who had less than she.

So, whilst Sophie Charlotte's brothers were being prepared to serve the duchy, the girls were being prepared to serve as-yet-unknown husbands. Their progress was monitored by their governess, Mademoiselle Seltzer, a noblewoman from the neighbouring Duchy of Württemberg[5] who had been childhood friends with Elisabeth Albertine. Mademoiselle Seltzer was virtually a member of the family and she oversaw the more feminine aspects of the girls' education that Gentmer could not, though she too spoke no English. Yet nobody suspected an ability to converse in English would be high on Sophie Charlotte's future agenda.

Effectively, Sophie Charlotte's early life resembled that of the landed but not quite monied gentry, rather than the mindbogglingly wealthy. The family revenues were a far from high-rolling £15,000 per year, less than half the annual allowance that one of her sons alone would later receive, but life in Mecklenburg was happy. The mornings were spent in lessons or bent over needlework and embroidery, skills Sophie Charlotte later shared with her own daughters. At the end of the morning, the two sisters would be taken for a walk or perhaps a drive before lunch. Then there was music, dancing, and household management to master. Years later, these would prove to be useful skills indeed.

It might all sound a little too good to be true, but Charlotte never forgot the unambitious, domesticated court of her youth. When Thomas Nugent, already famed for his extensive multi-volume account of his Grand Tour, visited Mirow, he painted a picture of a land where all was calm, a world away from the politicking court of England:

> They have no ambition here, but that of serving their prince and country; they idle not away their time, but act with the utmost diligence in their respective departments, they behave with a just dignity and decorum, avoiding the extremes of meanness and pride; they are content with their parental fortunes, which set them above the inordinate desire of riches; they are open and sincere, which renders them lovers of truth; they have no occasion to cringe to a prince whose aversion is flattery; they have the highest ideas of honour, and consequently are true to their engagements; they have an inviolable regard for all civil duties; they have a love for their prince on account of his virtues, and esteem him for his capacity: to conclude, it may be truly said that, instead of encouraging the ridicule of virtue, this court is a pattern of morality and religion, a school of probity and honour, a seminary of politeness, and in fine, the seat of every social virtue.
>
> This, my dear friend, is no exaggeration, but a fair portrait. The court of Strelitz, indeed, is not very numerous, but it is one of the most regular and most agreeable of any in the whole empire. No private family is governed with more order; and perhaps no prince is served by abler officers, and with greater diligence and affection.[6]

But this happy idyll wasn't destined to last. The Duke, who had always been a martyr to ill health, died in 1752 at the age of just 44. His death left his family heartbroken and the newly widowed Elisabeth Albertine came to rely ever more on the friendship of Mademoiselle Seltzer. Perhaps this was the genesis of the female circle that Sophie Charlotte herself later established, when she drew her daughters into a secretive cabal to which few men were admitted.

The Most Regular and Most Agreeable

Just months after the death of Sophie Charlotte's father, his reigning half-brother, Adolphus Frederick III, followed him to the grave. Because Adolphus Frederick left no male heir, the reigning dukedom descended to the next eligible member of the family: Adolphus Frederick IV, Sophie Charlotte's brother.

The new Duke of Mecklenburg-Strelitz was just 14 years old, so Elisabeth Albertine became her son's Regent. She packed up her whole household and the family moved from Mirow to the livelier world of Neustrelitz, which had been the capital of Mecklenburg-Strelitz since 1736.[7] For Elisabeth Albertine, however, a change of address didn't mean that other things had to change as well. The domestic and educational system that had worked so happily in Mirow continued in Neustrelitz, where the little group was joined by Frederike Elisabeth von Grabow, known to her charges as Madame de Grabow.

If Mademoiselle Seltzer was the perfect governess for the girls in their youth, as they grew older Madame de Grabow proved to be an ideal partner in the enterprise. The two women were already friends and Madame de Grabow enjoyed an excellent reputation as a poet, earning the admiring nickname, 'the German Sappho'. She was the daughter of the Mecklenburg minister at Vienna and a good marriage had left her a very rich widow. She fit into the household perfectly and became a firm favourite of the two princesses, whose love of geography was nurtured by their new governess's talent for cartography. Years later, when Sophie Charlotte was a queen, having played a part in her upbringing was Madame de Grabow's proudest achievement.

Although life in Neustrelitz was more formal than it had been in Mirow, Elisabeth Albertine went out of her way to ensure that there was as little disruption as possible to the familiar routine. Elisabeth Albertine was a firm believer in the old adage that the devil finds work for idle hands, and when the girls weren't in lessons, they were expected to indulge in improving pastimes. They never found their lessons a chore, in a large part because of their respect and affection for their tutors. In the years to come, the regime of schooling and self-improvement that had created Sophie Charlotte was very much in evidence for her children too. Unfortunately, they proved a little less receptive to it than she had been.

Sophie Charlotte was as sheltered as she ever had been, not yet joining her mother and older siblings when they dined in public, but every Sunday she was allowed to change out of her modest dresses and don her finest gown. She spent the morning in a long church service, then went out to tour the streets in a liveried coach pulled by six horses, accompanied by duchy guards. It was a very minor taste of the fame that would follow. This sheltered upbringing was also the basis of the life Sophie Charlotte's own daughters would one day be forced to live. They were kept away from the world for far longer than Sophie Charlotte ever was. The thought that she would eventually become one of the most famous women in Europe was unimaginable, and in a world where pushy mothers were always angling to grab the most prestigious spouse for their offspring that they could, Elisabeth Albertine had no such ambitions. What she wanted for them most of all was the same happiness that she had once known. It was no coincidence that life at her court was like that of a happy upper middle-class family, because she took pains to ensure that was exactly what she created.

Intelligent, affable, and taught to be humble, young Sophie Charlotte absorbed all of this like a sponge. If her mother's adherence to religious faith and humility was rather quaint in modern, forward-looking Germany, it was a fundamental building block in her daughter's personality. Even when she had the splendour of the British court at her fingertips, Sophie Charlotte held fast – sometimes infuriatingly so – to the lessons of piety and humility she had learned in childhood. They were qualities that the siblings seemed to share and when Sophie Charlotte's brother, Prince Charles Louis,[8] made a tour of the German courts, he received a marriage proposal from an anonymous but illustrious princess. She had all the qualifications that were considered essential in a wife, from pedigree and influence to wealth and beauty. Charles Louis, however, rejected the proposal for one reason: despite all her attributes, the princess was far too flippant when it came to religion. For the children of Elisabeth Albertine, this was beyond the pale.

May It Please Your Majesty

In many ways, life in Neustrelitz had been too good to last. Elisabeth Albertine had raised her children admirably and had devoted herself to ensuring that they enjoyed a childhood that wasn't only improving, but loving too. Whilst the major European courts were filled with drama and intrigue, in Neustrelitz there was precious little of either. Elisabeth Albertine knew that whilst her court might be happy, it was far from influential or particularly wealthy, so there was little point in hungrily pursuing the most illustrious bridegrooms for her daughters. Though she had proved to be an able Regent and her son was proving to be an able ruler, however, storm clouds were gathering. They would have a shattering effect on the court at Neustrelitz.

The first blows of the Seven Years' War were struck in 1756, when the Prussian armies of Frederick the Great invaded Saxony. Frederick had expected to form an alliance with the court of Mecklenburg-Schwerin but when none came, he turned his armies on the minor territories of the duchy and began to systematically punish them. It was inevitable that Neustrelitz would suffer.

Faced with the House of Mecklenburg's determination to remain neutral at all costs, Frederick the Great decided that, if he couldn't count on their support, then he would use them in another way. The ducal estates became the pathways along which vast numbers of his troops marched to reach their billets in the towns and villages dotted around the land. Though ostensibly neutral, Mecklenburg found its people and lands were treated with all the hostility that might be afforded to an enemy, and Frederick's troops behaved with all the terrifying might that one would expect of an occupying army. They helped themselves to what they wanted, when they wanted, pressganged men for the army, and taxed the people with reckless abandon. They took more than their share of food, occupied homes, and smashed up the furniture and belongings they found there to make firewood, leaving the citizens of the duchy starving, cold, and penniless. Though their conduct had supposedly not been ordered by the higher echelons within Prussia, a complete lack of censure or punishment suggested that whatever the troops were doing, they were doing with the blessing of their paymasters. In short, Frederick was punishing the duchy for its neutrality.

Eventually, the inevitable happened and Frederick the Great declared Mecklenburg a military garrison, from which his troops would defend Prussian interests against any attempts at incursion from Russia or Sweden. With seemingly no respite on the horizon, Elisabeth

Albertine sank into depression. She had the family's valuables packed up and smuggled to Hamburg to protect them from seizure by the Prussian military, but she was determined to stay on. To abandon her marital lands now, at their moment of greatest need, was something that Elisabeth Albertine couldn't countenance. Instead, she redoubled her efforts at philanthropy, but with the continent plunged into war, what little the Duchess could do was vastly outweighed by the daily torments visited on her subjects. The only hope left was that peace would soon break out, but that possibility seemed scant indeed.

Today we're well used to the PR games of celebrities, but it might come as a surprise to learn that in the eighteenth century, things weren't always so different. Long after the Prussian troops had left Mecklenburg and Sophie Charlotte had said *I do* to George III, a letter surfaced that ignited a fresh wave of affection for her. Though she was just a teenager when her ancestral lands fell into deprivation, legend had it that the young princess had penned an impassioned plea to Frederick the Great, begging him to withdraw his soldiers. The letter certainly appears to be straight from *someone's* heart, but it wasn't Sophie Charlotte's.

> May it please your Majesty,
> I am at a loss whether I should congratulate or condole
> with you on your late victory, since the same success
> which has covered you with laurels, has overspread
> the country of Mecklenburg with desolation. I know,
> Sire, that it seems unbecoming my sex, in this age of
> vicious refinement, to feel for one's country, to lament
> the horrors of war, or to wish for the return of peace.
> I know you may think it more properly my province
> to study the arts of pleasing, or to inspect subjects of
> a more domestic nature; but, however unbecoming it
> may be in me, I cannot resist the desire of interceding
> for this unhappy people.

It was but a very few years ago that this territory wore the most pleasing appearance. The country was cultivated, the peasant looked cheerful, and the towns abounded with riches and festivity. What an alteration, at present, from such a charming scene! I am not expert at describing, nor can my fancy add any horrors to the picture; but surely even conquerors themselves would weep at the prospect now before me. The whole country, my dear country, lies before me one frightful waste, presenting objects to excite terror, pity, and despair. The business of the husbandman and the shepherd are quite discontinued; the husbandman and the shepherd are become soldiers themselves, and assist to ravage the soil they formerly cultivated. The towns are inhabited only by old men, women, and children, with perhaps here and there a wounded and crippled warrior, left as useless at his own door. See how his little children come round him, ask the history of every wound, and grow almost soldiers themselves before they have judgment to calculate the distress that war brings upon mankind. But all this might be borne, did we not suffer from the alternate insolence of either army, as it happens to advance or retreat, in pursuing the objects of the campaign; it is impossible to express the confusion which those who even call themselves our friends create, and those from whom we might expect redress oppress us with new calamities. From your justice, Sire, it is, therefore, that we hope for relief; even women and children may complain to you, whose humanity stoops to the meanest petition, and whose power is capable of redressing the greatest injustice.

I am, Sire, &c.

Popular gossip after the marriage of Sophie Charlotte and George claimed that the letter had found its way to his mother, Augusta of Saxe-Gotha, Dowager Princess of Wales. The romantics explained that Augusta showed the letter to George II, who showed it to his grandson, who fell in love. Supposedly, rather like Prince Charming and Cinderella's slipper, when George II died and George III succeeded to the throne, he sent an envoy to Europe in search of the princess, with instructions not to rest until he had secured her hand in marriage.

Needless to say, that wasn't the case at all. Whoever wrote and circulated the letter, it certainly wasn't a young princess from Mecklenburg-Strelitz, but in the years to come she would be credited with Frederick the Great's decision to enforce military discipline amongst the troops stationed in Mecklenburg. Regardless of what was truly behind his decision, life in the duchy slowly began to settle down once more.

Far away in England, however, decisions were being taken that would change Sophie Charlotte's life forever. She little knew it, but a death in the royal family was on the cards.

The Boiling Youth

Over in England, meanwhile, a fatherless boy was being prepared to rule one of the superpowers of the eighteenth-century world. Frederick, the estranged son of George II, had died when his own son, also named George, was only 12, but during his lifetime he had been determined to present his family as the alternative take on the British monarchy. Fred knew the power of PR and he wasted no time in making himself a firm favourite with the public at the expense of his grumpy, bad-tempered father. Like George I and George II, Frederick had been born and raised in Germany, but he recognised the importance of playing up his son's very

British credentials. George was born in England and his parents made a very big deal indeed of making sure that everybody knew it. When Fred died, he left young a George a letter in which he told him, 'I shall have no regret never to have worn the crown, if you but fill it worthily. Convince the nation that you are not only an Englishman born and bred, but that you are also this by inclination.'

Fred's death catapulted young George to the head of the line of succession and his mother, Augusta of Saxe-Gotha, and grandfather, George II, were determined to protect him from ambitious fortune hunters. Intelligent and well-educated, but timid and suspicious by nature, George needed some training in what it took to be a monarch. Augusta searched for a suitable mentor for her son and found it in the shape of John Stuart, 3rd Earl of Bute. He had been a friend to her husband, and she charged him with preparing George for the massive duty that he would one day assume. Little did Augusta know that in doing so, she would open the door to rumours of favouritism, sexual intrigue, and cronyism that would dog her to her dying day.

Regardless of the suspicions of the public, Bute was soon a trusted companion of the young Prince of Wales. As he supervised George's transition from boy to man, George II and the Dowager Princess of Wales turned their attention to another matter. The prince, they knew, would soon need a wife, and the couple would need to be quick at producing an heir and more than a few spares. The young Prince of Wales had never been the healthiest of men, and few expected that he would live a long life.

The Prince of Wales was one of the most appealing morsels on offer to the ambitious brides of Europe, but his grandfather had already decided that the perfect candidate was Princess Sophie Caroline of Brunswick-Wolfenbüttel. She was the niece of Frederick the Great, with whom Britain had allied during the Seven Years' War, and a marriage between the two families would create an all-powerful alliance. In fact, the widowed George II was so fond of Sophie Caroline that he happily admitted he would have married her himself, had he been twenty years younger.

Augusta of Saxe-Gotha would have none of it. She was determined that her son could do far better, and she and Bute convinced the young prince of it too. Lord Waldegrave, the Prince's governor, wrote in his memoirs that:

> The Prince of Wales was taught to believe that he was to be made a Sacrifice merely to gratify the King's private Interest in the Electorate of Hanover. The young Princess was most cruelly misrepresented [:] all her Perfections were aggravated into Faults; and the Prince, without further Examination, was so willing to believe whatever could be invented to her disadvantage, that his Prejudice against her amounted almost to aversion itself.[9]

When George II saw his plans collapse, he bitterly remarked of his grandson, 'the boy [is] good for nothing, and only fit to read the bible to his mother.' Waldegrave went a step further, believing that, 'From this time, all Duty and Obedience to the Grandfather entirely ceas'd; for tho it would have been difficult to have persuaded him to have that which he thought wrong, he was ready to think right, whatever was prompted, either by the Mother or by her Favourite [Bute].'[10]

What the incident did teach George II was that Princess Augusta, who had always seemed to be an innocent in the thrall of her late husband, was a force to be reckoned with. George II was defeated and Augusta was determined that her niece, Frederica of Saxe-Gotha, would be the bride. To his mother's surprise, George turned her down, worried that Frederica's interest in philosophy was an early warning that she was trouble in waiting. Just like Sophie Charlotte, George valued faith above most things, and any bride who found philosophy fascinating was not the woman for him. Yet in his letters to Bute, the young prince revealed a different side of himself. Whilst his mother knew only of her pious and dutiful son, there was a lot going on under the surface. In a private letter, the 21-year-old George admitted to his worldly mentor that he struggled with:

> a daily encreasing [sic] admiration of the fair sex, which I am attempting with all the phylosophy [sic] and resolution I am capable of to keep under. I should be asham'd after having so long resisted the charms of these divine creatures now to become their prey. Princes when once in their hands make miserable figures [so] you will plainly feel how strong a struggle there is between the boiling youth of 21 years and prudence; the last I hope will ever keep the upper hand; indeed if I can weather it but a few years marriage will put a stop of this combat in my breast.[11]

'Could [George's mother] have chained up his body, as she had fettered his mind,' wrote Horace Walpole of that self-confessed *boiling youth*, 'It is probable she would have preferred his remaining single.'[12] But Augusta couldn't chain up her son and when it came to choosing the perfect bride, George was determined to play his part. He was also determined that, in order to avoid George II's interference, 'I can never consent to alter my [marital] situation whilst this Old Man lives; I will rather undergo anything ever so disagreeable than put my trust in him for a single moment in an affair of such delicacy.'[13] He didn't have long to wait, for the 'old man' had precious few months left to live.

Talk of a Wedding

> This morning about Seven o'Clock to the great Grief
> of an affectionate People, died his Most August
> Majesty George II, King and Parent of the British
> Dominions. His Majesty, it is said, expired in a Fit of
> Apoplexy, in the 77th Year of his Age, and 34th of his
> Reign.[14]

When the 22-year-old George III learned that he was King of
Great Britain, he swore to Bute that he would make the country
'the residence of true piety and virtue'. Now more than ever, he
needed to find a wife.

Across the nation, critics of the Dowager Princess of Wales
feared that she and Bute were the puppet masters who would
control the new young king, but the fact that Augusta hadn't been
able to impose Frederica of Saxe-Gotha signalled that this wasn't
the case. Though George would always be close to his mother and
future prime minister Bute, when it came to marriage, the young
monarch was determined that the decision should be his. In fact,
he already knew the perfect candidate.

She was Lady Sarah Lennox, the daughter of the Duke of
Richmond. The young Lady Sarah had been a favourite at the
court of King George II but as far as Augusta was concerned,
she was far from ideal. Lady Sarah might have been intelligent,
accomplished, pretty, and of noble birth, but she was a long
way from royal. Still, Lady Sarah and the king had spent years
making doe-eyes at one another and he seemed set on her. To
help his cause, he enlisted their mutual friend, Lady Susan Fox-
Strangeways, to drop hints to the young lady concerned.

'They talk of a wedding,' George told Lady Susan. 'I think an
English match would do better than a foreign one. Pray tell Lady
Sarah Lennox I said so.'[15] The implication was obvious: Lady Sarah

should know that the young sovereign was seeking an English bride, because she was the English bride he wanted.

When she got wind of it, the Dowager Princess of Wales was furious. In order to upset her son's romantic aims, she employed both her eldest daughter, Augusta, and Lady Bute, the wife of George's mentor, to throw a spanner into the works. The two women inveigled themselves into any gathering at which Lady Sarah was present and, whilst Augusta openly mocked Sarah's attachment to the king, Lady Bute played the part of a friend, winkling out gossip and sending it back to the Princess of Wales. Henry Fox, the ambitious Whig grandee, was equally keen to ensure that Lady Sarah, whose family were his long-time political opponents, didn't gain a footing. His master plan was to get the king out of the way with a trip to the coast, hoping that putting some distance between George and the object of his affections would do the trick. Instead, the Lennox family simply followed him. Each day, when George took the air on horseback, Lady Sarah appeared 'in a field close to the great road,' wrote Horace Walpole, 'making hay.'[16]

In an effort to distract George, Bute entrusted the Hanoverian minister in London, Baron Philipp Adolphus von Münchausen, with the task of making discreet matchmaking enquiries in Germany. The lucky lady should be of royal birth, ideally German, and she must be a Protestant, as no reigning monarch or heir was permitted to marry a Roman Catholic on pain of seeing their children booted out of the line of succession. Augusta and George alike both wanted a wife who was unlikely to take an interest in politics too. For George, this was because he didn't want to be perceived as a king whose decisions were made by his queen. In the case of his mother, it was because she and Bute held an unparalleled amount of influence over the young king, and she wasn't about to sacrifice it to a newly arrived bride.

By now recognising that his mother would never consent to his marrying Lady Sarah Lennox, George grudgingly examined the list of potential brides. He didn't like what he saw. 'Our evening has been spent looking in the New Berlin Almanack for Princesses where three new ones have been found, as yet unthouht [sic] of,'[17] he told Bute. The search was on. As it gathered pace, Lady Sarah Lennox confided in a friend that her disappointment wasn't too great because, she 'did not love [George], and only liked him'. Lady Sarah soon moved on and accepted the end of her marital hopes without complaint.[18] What else could she do, after all?

An Amiable Character

'The king's longing and impatience increase daily,'[19] wrote Baron von Münchausen, and Lady Sarah was right there on the scene, should his impatience get the better of him. Yet as far as the rest of the world and Horace Walpole knew, 'of a Queen, the talk is dropped; and no other changes are likely to be made yet.'[20] In fact, it was anything but dropped, yet the enquiries were more discreet than ever, and the pool of candidates was shrinking.

Elisabeth Albertine considered the chances of her daughter, Sophie Charlotte, so remote that she had already made arrangements for her to be admitted to a convent. This was no austere sanctuary, as Charlotte herself told Frances Burney many years later. 'They have balls,' confided the scandalised queen. 'Not at home, but next door, and there is no restriction, but to go to prayers at eight, at nine, and at night – that is very little you know – and wear black or white.'[21] For a woman who held her faith in such high regard, it would have been unthinkable.

As Sophie Charlotte was receiving the cross that was the first stage of her admission to convent life, the search for a queen was heating up. Münchausen's brother, Baron Gerlach Adolphus, sat at the pinnacle of Hanoverian government, and his opinion of the women on the list was sought. George had already removed some of the suggestions and Münchausen put paid to the hopes of others, some because of scandals in the family, others because of ill health and concerns about their fertility. When Münchausen returned the list to his brother, he had added a candidate of his own. That candidate was Princess Sophie Charlotte of Mecklenburg-Strelitz.

In early January, George, Bute, and Münchausen settled down to examine the four princesses who still remained on the list: Schwedt, Darmstadt, Brunswick, and Strelitz. Appended to it were notes by Münchausen's brother-in-law, Major Von Schulenburg, who had personal knowledge of each princess. Brunswick was dismissed as too young, and Schwedt as too bad-tempered. Of Darmstadt little was known, and the men determined that more investigation should be undertaken if possible. When this investigation confirmed that 'the Princess's mother told very lately that she is stubborn and ill temper'd to the greatest degree',[22] her chances grew considerably fainter. The final straw came when George learned that her father was considered to be under the malign influence of occultists, who 'have brought the Prince very near to the borders of madness'.[23] George baulked, concerned at the reports that had 'given me such melancholy thoughts of what may perhaps be in the blood'.[24] Only Sophie Charlotte now remained to be considered.

In many ways, Sophie Charlotte was the perfect candidate to marry George, whilst in other ways, she was far from ideal. As the little-known daughter of a minor German duchy, she was untouched by scandal or politics, but that meant there was a risk that she was simply not cut out for the job. Being a queen required a very specific sort of education and an understanding of protocol and duty, as well as the right character. The king assured Bute that he was particularly heartened by a report from Münchausen's niece 'giving a very amiable character to the P[rincess] of Strelitz;

he says that the Princess has very good sense; if that is the case a little of England's air will soon give her the deportment necessary for a British Queen.'[25]

Münchausen thought her chances were so unlikely that he hadn't even sent her portrait to the king, but as the list was whittled down still further, it was Sophie Charlotte to whom George kept returning. Finally, the self-confessed *boiling youth* received the portrait and made his decision.

'I own, 'tis not in every particular as I could wish,' he told Bute, 'But yet I am resolved to fix here.'[26] Subject to a few final appraisals of Sophie Charlotte's character, the king had made up his mind. That he had done it all without mentioning his plans to Sophie Charlotte or her mother was merely symptomatic of the royal marriage market.

Nature Has Been Bountiful

With the king's interest in Sophie Charlotte now seemingly fixed, he needed one final opinion on the lady who would be queen. For this most important of tasks, Bute selected his old friend Colonel David Graeme, a former Jacobite sympathiser. Graeme took off for the continent, where he came upon the Duchess and her daughters taking the waters at Pyrmont. This was an extraordinary stroke of good fortune for the Scot, who was able to blend into the background and observe Sophie Charlotte unnoticed. Like this, he would be able to see how she really behaved, unaware that an envoy from the British court was keeping a keen eye on her. What he saw pleased him. She was good-natured, impeccably behaved, and utterly unobtrusive, but there was one potential sticking point. Charlotte loved to play cards and was generally very successful at it; she was also, Graeme suspected, a bad loser, who always looked deeply put out if she didn't claim the victory. Graeme interpreted this as a worrying indication that the princess was avaricious, but there was an associated mystery that intrigued him. Whenever Sophie Charlotte had enjoyed a successful night at the gaming table, she was absent for a considerable portion of the following morning. One day, the colonel's curiosity got the better of him and he secretly followed Sophie Charlotte on her morning walk.

To Graeme's surprise, Sophie Charlotte spent the morning distributing her winnings between Pyrmont's poor. The princess's excitement at winning wasn't for her own benefit at all, it was because of the charitable good she might do with the money. In short, she was everything that George III was looking for in a wife.

Graeme went on to Neustrelitz when the party left Pyrmont, arriving in June and carrying with him a letter from the Dowager Princess of Wales. In it, Augusta explained that she was seeking an opportunity to unite their two families, but it would depend entirely on the response of the Dowager Duchess Elisabeth Albertine to some questions she had enclosed. Until then, cautioned the Princess of Wales, the king should not be considered to have made any commitment to the princess. With her health failing, the Duchess employed Princess Christiane to act as her mouthpiece, assuring Graeme that her eldest daughter was entirely to be trusted.

By now just weeks from death, Elisabeth Albertine replied to Augusta's letter and assured her that Sophie Charlotte was and never had been a Roman Catholic, but was instead a Lutheran. She assured her also that the young princess had neither followers nor previous betrothals in her past. If all was to the liking of the British court, wrote Christiane on her weakened mother's behalf, then Sophie Charlotte would be ready to leave for England by the start of August. Finally, as Elisabeth Albertine signed the letter, Sophie Charlotte was brought to her mother's sickbed and informed of George III's interest in her. She indicated, according to Graeme, 'her willingness to submit to what might be required of her',[27] demonstrating that placid obedience that has erroneously become so associated with Queen Charlotte.

Colonel Graeme dispatched the letter without delay and added to it his own report on the princess. These were the papers that would decide the fate of the royal bride-to-be:

> The complexion of the Princess is delicate and fine, with abundance of red, not to be called a high bloom; but as much as, in my opinion, there should be at her age and sufficient to relevate [sic] the lustre of a very fine white.
>
> Her hair is a pale brown, more than *cendré*; well enough set, but rather advancing a little too much upon the face at the upper part of the temples; the whole head is fine hair and dresses well. Her nose good, and *not flat*, though at a little distance there is somewhat of that appearance, which is expressed in the picture which H.M. was pleased to show me: that appearance of flatness is rather a narrowness across the eyes, with a prominence of the upper lip, together with a widening of the lower part of the face; the back part of the cheek especially very well turned, with a very good mixture of red and white. The mouth rather large; and as the French express it *pas trop bien fondu...*
>
> To sum up all, I shall say of the Princess, she is not a beauty but what is little inferior, she is *amiable*, and her face rather agreeable than otherwise.
>
> The Princess is rather above the middle size, and promises to be taller still. The appearance of her person is not quite that of a woman fully formed, nor may it be expected at her age, though the bosom is full

enough for her age and person. She has the appearance of good health, and I am told enjoys a very constant and uninterrupted state of it. The whole figure straight, genteel and easy, all her actions and carriage natural and unaffected, marking a great goodness of health with a deal of candour and ingenuity...

Though nature has been bountiful enough in bestowing upon her very good qualities and talents, I cannot say that these have been cultivated with the care they merited, but as she is so very young I think she is capable of taking any impression, or being moulded into any form.

Between them, Colonel Graeme's report and Elisabeth Albertine's letter sealed the deal. On 1 July 1761, George wrote a letter to Bute in which he said cheerily that Graeme's 'letter removes any difficultys [sic], and will enable as soon as my Dearest Friend thinks proper (which I hope will be immediately) to declare the affair.'[28] George was keen for Sophie Charlotte to be a married woman before the Coronation, which was planned for September. He didn't, however, want her to be plunged into that particular circus without having some breathing space first. He wrote to Bute again, signalling the urgency that should be applied to the matter:

The more I revolve in my mind the affair, the more I wish to have it immediately concluded; the state of the Dutchesses [sic] health, my friends wishing to have the Coronation in September, are additional reasons for dispatch, for how disagreable [sic] would it not be for a young person to appear almost at her first arrival in Westminster Abbey and go through all that ceremony, besides contrary winds might detain

her, and consequently force that august ceremony to
be suspended, which would be very irregular, and
disappointed thousands who will be flocking on this
occasion to London; indeed she ought to be above a
month here before that day that she may have a little
recover'd that first bashfulness which is beautiful in
her first appearance; I must on this occasion make use
of a favourite expression of the *Man Mountain* [Pitt]
that willing minds overcome all difficulties; I will
engage every thing that shall be so prepar'd that she
may be here by the 10th of August.[29]

Bute shared the news of George's forthcoming nuptials with a
very select group of three. They were Thomas Pelham-Holles,
Duke of Newcastle and prime minister, William Pitt, Secretary of
State for the South, and the 1st Earl of Hardwicke, Philip Yorke,
one of the prime minister's closest advisors and former Lord High
Chancellor.

Amid great secrecy, plans were made for Sophie Charlotte to
leave behind the only life she had known and travel thousands of
miles to become a queen. Whilst sensitive to her situation, George
laid some ground rules that she must follow from the off. One of
them, sadly for Sophie Charlotte, was that she should not expect
to bring a whole cavalcade of familiar faces. Marriages might be
about romance – sometimes – but in the royal courts, they were
about diplomacy too.

'As to who she may bring, that is a clear point, this country
very wisely not admitting foreigners to hold appointments,'
George wrote to Bute, who conveyed the message to Graeme.
'The utmost she can bring is one or two Feme's [sic] de
Chambres, which I own I hope will be quiet people, for by my
own experience I have seen these women meddle much more
than they ought to do.'[30]

The king announced his engagement to an extraordinary meeting of the Privy Council on 8 July.

> Having nothing so much at Heart, as to procure the Welfare, and Happiness of My People, and to render the same stable, and permanent, to Posterity … I am come to a Resolution to demand in Marriage the Princess Charlotte of Mecklenburg Strelitz, a Princess distinguished by every eminent Virtue and amiable Endowment, whose Illustrious Line has constantly shewn the firmest Zeal for the Protestant Religion, and a particular Attachment to My Family.[31]

The wheels of marriage were in motion.

What Food for Newsmongers

> An extraordinary Privy Council of all the members in and near town was summoned by the King's own messengers, not by those of the Council, to meet *on the most urgent and important* business … To declare a queen. *Urgent* business enough, I believe; I do not see how it was *important*. The handkerchief has been tossed a vast way; it is to a Charlotte, Princess of Mecklenbourg [sic]; Lord Harcourt is to be at her father's Court – if he can find it, on the first of August, and the coronation of both their Majesties is fixed for the 22nd of September. What food for newsmongers, tattle, solicitations, mantua-makers, jewellers, &c., for above two months to come![32]

When Horace Walpole wrote to Horace Mann with his characteristic blend of waspish gossip and current affairs, he was sharing some of the hottest news in Europe. He was wrong to state that the tiny court was that of Sophie Charlotte's *father*, of course, but in all other respects his information was reliably accurate, right down to the snipe regarding the tiny size of the duchy. It was to that little territory that Lord Harcourt, the king's former governor who was later to become Sophie Charlotte's Master of the Horse, had been sent.

By the time Lord Harcourt left for Neustrelitz, Princess Sophie Charlotte was an orphan. Her mother had never recovered from the illness that had left her bedridden and barely able to speak during Colonel Graeme's visit. She died on 29 June 1761, aged just 47 years old. Heartbroken by the death of her mother, Sophie Charlotte was glad of the worldly colonel's presence and when Graeme sought assurances on the king's behalf that she would have no qualms about observing the rites of the Church of England, she assured him that she would not. She was as keen to see the marriage progress as her husband-to-be, but likely not for the same reasons. Germany was suffering a heatwave and Elisabeth Albertine's death had been followed by the hasty removal of her body to the ducal chapel, where it was buried under sand until the funeral could begin. The once happy home was gripped by mourning and Sophie Charlotte was devastated, but even the talk of marriage brought sadness. Charlotte's elder sister, Princess Christiane, had fallen in love with the Duke of Roxburghe during the latter's visit to Germany, and he was head over heels for her too. The couple hoped to be married but the marriage contract of George and Sophie Charlotte stipulated that Christiane, as sister of the British queen, was forbidden from marrying a British subject. As a result, she and Roxburghe were forced to part despite their love. Neither ever married.

Intriguingly, there has been debate among historians as to whether Sophie Charlotte and George were married by proxy before she left Mecklenburg. According to the recollections of

Sophia Stuart, the Earl of Bute's daughter-in-law, Sophie Charlotte was summoned to dinner by her mother and brother, and told she would be sitting beside an ambassador from the British court. She was advised to dress in her finest gown and jewels and to make the best impression she could. Sophie Charlotte had no idea that she was being considered as a bride for the young king, but she did as she was told and made polite conversation with the visitors from the court of George III. She must have been a hit during the meal because once the plates were cleared, Sophie Charlotte was in for the surprise of her life.

> The folding-doors flew open to the saloon, which she saw splendidly illuminated; and there appeared a table, two cushions, and everything prepared for a wedding. Her brother then gave her his hand; and, leading her in, used his favourite expression:- '*Allons, ne faites pas l'enfant – tu vas être Reine d'Angleterre.*'[33] … They knelt down. The ceremony, whatever it was, proceeded. She was laid on the sofa, upon which he laid his foot; and they all embraced her, calling her, '*la Reine.*'[34]

There are several clues in Sophia Stuart's account that suggest it is not accurate. Dowager Duchess Elisabeth Albertine was bedridden and nearing death during Colonel Graeme's visit. She was in no state to attend a formal dinner and proxy wedding, nor to help her daughter dress and accessorise with jewels from her own collection, as stated elsewhere in Stuart's recollections. Secondly, there is little mention of any negotiations, let alone those carried out by Colonel Graeme. Stuart also claimed that Elisabeth Albertine hoped to accompany Sophie Charlotte to the coast for her journey to England. This would have been impossible, since the Dowager Duchess was dead by the time her daughter left for Neustrelitz.

So if Stuart's memory was misleading, what of the proxy wedding ceremony? The ducal court was far from wealthy and a proxy wedding was by necessity an expensive affair, needing ceremony, gifts, and pomp, not to mention that a wedding would immediately transform Princess Sophie Charlotte into Queen Charlotte. In that case, she would have been expected to establish an entire queen's entourage who would travel with her to England. This would have entailed even more expense for her cash-strapped family court, and flown in the face of George III's stipulation that she should bring only a couple of attendants. It's far more likely that there was no proxy wedding, and that Sophie Charlotte was still a princess when she boarded the royal yacht. *The Royal Charlotte* had until recently been *The Royal Caroline*, and it had been refurbished and opulently gilded at an eyewatering cost.

In England, Lord Harcourt set out for Europe in the company of the Duchess of Ancaster, the Duchess of Hamilton, Lady Effingham, and Harcourt's son, William, who would be Sophie Charlotte's equerry. It was up to the king to assemble his future wife's household, in which Colonel Graeme would serve as Secretary and later Comptroller. It was hardly surprising that a friend wryly told the former Jacobite, 'Colonel Graeme, I congratulate you on exchanging the dangerous employment of making kings, for the more lucrative one of making queens.'

But Graeme had won Sophie Charlotte's trust by the kindness and understanding he showed on the death of her mother. It was he who obtained the princess's measurements so a whole new wardrobe could be made in anticipation of her arrival. A fortune in jewels would also be waiting, and the royal couple would celebrate their nuptials in a newly renovated suite in St James's Palace. All was going swimmingly until George learned that Lord Harcourt had taken it upon himself to permit Sophie Charlotte to bring her personal hairdresser to England. Even this was one German too many for his liking. He had gone to pains to prove he was an *English* king, don't forget, and George was nothing if not set in his ways.

> I have just receiv'd [from Graeme] a lock of the Princesses hair, which seems at candle of a very fine dark colour, and very soft; I can't help expressing a little surprise on Lord Harcourt and Greehm [sic] bringing over a hair dresser when the orders were so very positive that only two women were to come; had the Princess said anything, that might perhaps have been a reason for their acting as they now have done.[35]

On this matter, though, George relented. Sophie Charlotte would be permitted to bring her *frizzeur* to her new home. Hair was the one thing on which the new queen proved to be immovable. Though she readily exchanged her German gowns for British dresses, 'On the road they wanted to curl her toupet,' wrote Horace Walpole. 'She said she thought it looked as well as that of any of the ladies sent to fetch her; if the King bid her, she would wear a periwig, otherwise she would remain as she was.'[36]

The Destiny of the British Nation

Lord Harcourt made for Neustrelitz with all the speed he could muster, a miniature of King George III set with diamonds carried safely in his luggage. Eager to meet his bride, the monarch managed every bit of Harcourt's task personally, from his departure to his return, with Sophie Charlotte safely in his custody. She would be received at Gravesend by the Lord Chamberlain, William Cavendish, 4th Duke of Devonshire, who would mark the occasion by kissing her hand when she disembarked from the royal yacht. This was at the personal request of the king, who told him, 'Nobody shall kiss her hand till she is Queen, except my Lord Chamberlain, and you must, when you first see her.'

Still in mourning for her late mother, Princess Sophie Charlotte had no say in any of it. Nor did she have any say in the appointment of the Duchess of Ancaster as her Mistress of the Robes, or the Duke of Manchester as her Chamberlain. The Duchess of Hamilton, Lady Effingham, Lady Northumberland, Lady Weymouth, and Lady Bolingbroke were all appointed to the team of twelve ladies-in-waiting on the say so of her bridegroom too. Nor would Sophie Charlotte have any part to play in the employment of a legion of pages, ushers, physicians, coachmen, musicians, and others who would make up her vast household. She would even leave behind the name she had used her whole life. Her Serene Highness Sophie Charlotte would henceforth be known as Charlotte, a name fit for a queen.

Lord Harcourt arrived at Neustrelitz in the full bloom of summer to find excitement at a fever pitch. With him, he carried the marriage treaty that would seal the princess's fate. He found her in a state of nervous excitement, grief at the loss of her mother tangled with anticipation for what was to come. Graeme had been a rock to the princess since her bereavement and Harcourt was immensely pleased at what he found. He wrote that 'Our Queen, that is to be, has seen very little of the world, but her very good sense, vivacity, and cheerfulness, I dare say, will recommend her to the King and make her the darling of the British nation. … In short, she is a very fine girl.'[37]

All that was left now were the formalities. Lord Harcourt officially delivered the king's proposal on the morning of 15 August, and Princess Charlotte officially accepted. As soon as the marriage contract had been signed by Harcourt and the First Marshall of the Court of Strelitz, Count Frederick Zesterfleth, the cannons fired to signal that the happy event was now confirmed, and Charlotte made a short speech of thanks. Charmed, Harcourt predicted, 'No marriage can afford a greater prospect of happiness.'

It was with a sense of a job well done that he joined the princess and more than 150 illustrious guests for a lavish celebratory banquet that spread across three apartments in the ducal palace. More than 40,000 lamps lit the town, and a grand festival was held so that the people might celebrate their princess's betrothal too. For a relatively humble court, on this occasion Neustrelitz turned up in style.

Two days after the signing of the marriage treaty, Charlotte left Neustrelitz for good in the company of the party from England, her sister, and her brother, the 'young Prince of Mecklenburg Strelitz', who had benefitted already from his new familial connections and been 'promoted to the Rank of a General in the Hanoverian service'.[38] Charlotte's brothers would become regular visitors to her new kingdom, gaining plaudits and accruing debts that Charlotte was often called upon to settle.

Charlotte's voyage to the coast and the royal yacht that awaited her now began. She travelled in a magnificent procession to the borders of the town and on through her brother's territory, stopping first at Altstrelitz, where she passed beneath a triumphal arch festooned with innumerable flowers and topped by the arms of Strelitz and England. As Charlotte's Hanoverian state coach passed through, twelve girls in white gowns and flower crowns, each holding a ceremonial myrtle wreath, formed an honour guard on either side of the road. They recited a verse of congratulations before the burgomaster, Tangatz, read a farewell address to the princess. Charlotte thanked the people profusely and seemed particularly enchanted by the little girls, who scattered their wreaths on the ground as the party resumed its arduous journey towards the coast.

The next stop was Mirow, where Charlotte bade farewell to those familiar faces who had cared for her in childhood. The party then passed into Prignitz and Perleberg, where she made a generous gift to the Prussians who escorted her. Charlotte's next stop was over the Elbe at Göhrde, once the beloved hunting lodge of George I. Here, in her fiancé's ancestral lands, she grew further accustomed to her new life in the public eye. After two dinners in public and a walk through the park before fascinated spectators, it was back into the carriage and off to Stade, where an enormous crowd was waiting. Noblewomen presented an exhausted Charlotte with congratulatory verses that rested on rich velvet cushions, whilst lanterns lit the town and triumphal arches were raised above the main streets to celebrate the forthcoming royal nuptials. Overwhelmed, Charlotte gasped, 'Can I be worthy of all these honours?' She finally reached Cuxhaven in the last week of August, where George, Admiral Lord Anson – memorably referred to by Horace Walpole as 'the king's chief eunuch' – would command the fleet that was to carry the new queen to England.

As her new English attendants waited aboard the royal yacht, Charlotte finally said goodbye to the remaining friends who had travelled with her from Strelitz. Only her hairdresser, Frederick Albert Papendiek,[39] who would become a page, and two attendants, Juliana Elizabeth von Schwellenberg, who had been in Charlotte's retinue since childhood, and Johanna Louisa Hagedorn, were permitted to complete the journey with their mistress. It's not hard to imagine what trepidation was going through Charlotte's mind as she looked upon the scene of chaos that waited on the harbour, where one Prussian eyewitness remembered that everything was

> in confusion – servants running about with luggage, and waiting-women only half dressed, with garments over their arms which in their haste they had not got packed. Finally came along an Englishwoman with an immense green taffety bag, containing the dress the Princess is to wear when she meets the king; the woman was showing it to everybody who wanted to see it.

Charlotte then climbed aboard one of the freshly refitted boats and was ferried out to the *Royal Charlotte*. As a band began to play and the guns roared a salute, she stole a last look back at the world she had known. Her life, sheltered and insular as it was, would never be the same again. When the British duchesses knelt before her, Charlotte assured them that she already looked on them as friends. It augured well for life in England.

Even at this early stage, Charlotte showed some of the steel that she would later exhibit when dealing with her errant sons and ailing husband. Rather than fret or grieve, she went immediately to the deck and paid homage to the sailors who had gathered on the surrounding ships to see her. Charlotte, it seemed, was blessed with an eye for public relations. The British press were filled with enthusiasm for their incoming queen too, painting a picture of a young lady 'of a middling size, rather inclining to tall, a fine shape, graceful carriage, fine neck and hands, brown hair, round face, blue eyes, mouth rather large, rosy lips, and extreme fine teeth, which appear when she smiles or speaks'.[40]

The voyage to England was hazardous and difficult, lashed by storms and crashing waves. Yet even as the sailors battled through the tempest, Charlotte maintained her temper. As one magazine noted, contrary to the two duchesses who were laid low with seasickness, Charlotte 'was not at all affected with the storm, but bore the sea like a truly British Queen'.[41] She played her harpsichord, rehearsed her groom's favourite English melodies and the National Anthem, and chatted amiably – in French, of course – with her new retainers. But Charlotte wasn't content to rest on her laurels when it came to language. Well aware of her fiancé's dedication to his British realms, as the vessel was battered by the wind and waves Charlotte took shelter in her cabin, passing the time practising her English. During their first months of marriage, George often attended his wife's English lessons and encouraged her along. She wore only English gowns too, absolutely set on making the right impression.

Each time it seemed as though the fleet might be able to reach its destination, high winds drove it back out to sea. Eventually, it was decided that the carefully laid plans for Charlotte to land at Greenwich must be abandoned. 'Fresh orders have been sent to Lord Anson,' observed Lloyd's Evening Post, 'to land the Princess Sophia Charlotte of Mecklenburgh [sic], our intended Queen, at any port of Great Britain he can first make to.'[42] On receipt of these orders, the fleet made for Harwich, where they stood a far better chance of successfully reaching dry land. When the royal yacht was finally sighted, a messenger was sent to bring word to the increasingly desperate king that the danger was ended. The Coronation of 22 September would have its queen.

Overjoy'd to the Greatest Degree

When word reached George III that Charlotte was safely in sight of the coast after ten perilous days at sea, he was overjoyed. He had watched the weather with increasing concern since she set out from Cuxhaven, mindful not just of the dangers posed by the storms, but of the immovable Coronation that loomed on the horizon. Late that evening he wrote to Lord Bute, filled with hope for the future.

> I now think my domestic happiness in my own power, I am overjoy'd to the greatest degree and very impatient for that minute that joins me to her, I hope for my life; I cannot too much return my sincere and humble acknowledgements to my Creator for this greatest blessing that he has been pleased to point out to me.
>
> I have now but one wish as a public man and that is that He will make her fruitful.[43]

What a relief it must have been for Charlotte to finally feel solid ground beneath her feet again. By the end of the voyage, even her indomitable spirit had begun to flag, and it was a tired princess who was received by the mayor and aldermen of Harwich. She spent the night at the Grove, the seat of the Earl of Abercorn, where mealtimes brought another taste of the regal life as the door was left open so that people could watch the future queen dine. The following day, after calling on a wine merchant at Rumford for coffee, Charlotte climbed into the king's coach with the Duchesses of Ancaster and Hamilton, and the party began the final stage of its journey.

At every step, crowds pressed forward hoping to see her. Some got more than they bargained for:

> On Tuesday last, as the Queen was coming to Town, near Bow, a Servant to a Gentleman in that Neighbourhood was so indiscrete as to lay his Hand on the Window of the Coach, and jump up, for which he had his fingers terribly cut with a Broad-Sword by one of the Guards.[44]

When she had left Cuxhaven, Charlotte was still a German princess, but now she was every inch an English queen, in a gown of gold brocade accented with diamonds. She bade the driver to go slowly so that the gathered crowds might see her, and she them. Though Charlotte smiled and waved to her new subjects as she passed, the more worldly Duchess of Hamilton could see that her young charge's nerves were beginning to show. Walpole confided in his friend, General Thomas Conway, that:

> When she caught the first glimpse of the palace, she grew frightened and turned pale. The Duchess of Hamilton smiled – the princess said, 'My dear duchess, you may laugh: you have been married twice,

but it is no joke to me.' Her lips trembled as the coach stopped, but she jumped out with spirit, and has done nothing but with good humour and cheerfulness.[45]

On 8 September 1761, Princess Charlotte finally found herself at the gates of St James's Palace. She was helped from her carriage by the Duke of Devonshire and received by the Duke of York, who caught the nervous princess in a stumble. As his bride steadied herself, the king descended the steps from the palace to meet her. Overcome by the moment and keen to observe protocol, Charlotte went to throw herself to the ground at his feet, but George was having none of it. Instead, wrote Lady Kildare, aunt of Lady Sarah Lennox, 'he raised her up, embraced her and led her thro' the garden up the steps into the palace.'[46]

Charlotte was welcomed into St James's Palace by a groom who was truly delighted to see her. She offered him her snuff box as a friendly gesture and, upon the king's gentle reply that he never touched the stuff, Charlotte immediately abandoned her beloved snuff to her attendant with a promise that she would never use it again. Days later, in recognition of her gesture, George presented his bride with not one but two extravagant snuffboxes, each encrusted with diamonds. On one was a miniature of his portrait, on the other a miniature of hers.

The signs couldn't have been better. In just a few hours, Charlotte would be a married queen, but the first order of the day was to introduce her to her new family and the ten bridesmaids – Lady Sarah Lennox included – who would attend her, 'whipped on their virginity', according to Walpole. George introduced her first to his mother, then to his siblings and other relations. Only then, once she had met everybody, was the wide-eyed Charlotte shown to her rooms to prepare for the evening ahead.

The night was hot and sultry as the bride-to-be was laced into her wedding finery by her assistant dressers, Miss Laverocke and Miss Pascall, under the watchful eye of the Duchess of Ancaster,

Mistress of the Robes. Charlotte's dress, which she wore again for her Coronation, was heavy, sweltering, and too big for her petite frame. It was also every bit as grand as one might expect for a queen.

> A silver tissue, stiffen bodied gown, embroidered & trimmed with silver. On her head a little Cap of purple Velvet quite covered with Diamonds, a Diamond Aigrette in the form of a Crown, 3 dropped Diamond Earrings, Diamond Necklace, Diamond Sprigs of Flowers on her Sleeves and to clasp back her Robe, a diamond Stomacher, her purple Velvet Mantle was laced with Gold and lined with Ermine.[47]

George's wedding gift to his wife was a treasure trove of jewels, and coming from the relatively humble court of Mecklenburg-Strelitz, it's not hard to imagine the wonder with which Charlotte received them. Jewellery was to remain one of the queen's lifelong vices, though she fretted endlessly about the value of her collection. 'I thought at first I should always choose to wear them,' she told Frances Burney. 'But the fatigue and trouble of putting them on, and the care they required, and the fear of losing them, believe me, ma'am, in a fortnight's time I longed again for my earlier dress.' Charlotte's critics didn't believe a word of it, and accusations of avarice were levelled at her until her dying day. Stories such as that of a magnificent collection of diamonds received from a Nabob in return for the gift of a lion did her no favours whatsoever.

> The King's particular present to his bride was a pair of bracelets, consisting of six rows of picked pearls as large as a full pea; the clasps – one his picture, the other his hair and cypher, both set round with diamonds; necklace with diamond cross; earrings, and the additional ornaments of the fashion of the

day. Also a diamond hoop ring of a size not to stand higher than the wedding ring, to which it was to serve as a guard. On that finger the Queen never allowed herself to wear any other in addition, although fashion at times almost demanded it.[48]

In the years to come, Queen Charlotte came to treasure her wedding ring and the diamond hoop, which George had had engraved with the date of their marriage, as though they were holy relics. They were the symbols of a union that had once seemed utterly unbreakable – something virtually unheard of for the Georgian kings.

Though Charlotte's gown and jewels were fabulous, they were impractical too. The heavy fabric and piles of gemstones caused an unfortunate wardrobe malfunction as her mantle, 'fastened on her shoulder by a bunch of large pearls, dragged itself and almost the rest of her clothes halfway down her waist'.[49] It was hardly what a bride needed in front of a crowd. The court in Charlotte's homeland had been small but here in London it was vast, and as the Duke of York escorted her through the palace to dinner with the royal family, she blanched as the courtiers pressed closer to get a look at her. 'Courage,' York urged gently, 'courage.'

Fortunately for Charlotte, her husband's family were determined to make her feel at home. She misunderstood that she was expected to allow the female courtiers to kiss her hand and started in alarm until George's unimpressed sister, Princess Augusta, reluctantly took her hand and lifted it to show Charlotte what was expected of the queen.

Finally, as 10.00 pm approached, the wedding party made its way towards the Chapel Royal. Ten women carried the princess's opulent purple train and the Duke of York walked alongside her, passing through a guard of honour as trumpets blared to announce her arrival. When Charlotte and George stood together before the altar, the bride was silent as the Archbishop of Canterbury read the wedding vows. Only when she was required to answer '*Ich will*' in her native tongue did Charlotte say so much as a word.

> The Marriage Ceremony began at Nine at Night; at the Conclusion of which, the Guns at the Park and the Tower were fired, and the Cities of London and Westminster, &c, finely illuminated. The Rejoycings were universally expressed by the People, with that Chearfulness which true Loyalty inspires on the happy Occasion.[50]

Immediately after the wedding ceremony, as the royal couple greeted their guests, the streets of London erupted into celebrations. At last Charlotte seemed to be settling in, even going so far as to play the harpsichord and sing for the assembled guests. It was a great way to make the best sort of impression. Even after the clock had struck midnight, Charlotte toured the room, chatting excitedly to guests until Princess Augusta decided that the time had come to break up the party. Seeing how tired his sister was, George delicately informed his new wife that it was time for bed.

According to tradition, the newlyweds should have been escorted to their bedchamber, where the business of making heirs and spares was expected to get underway. This, however, was a step too far for Charlotte. At her request, the ceremony was abandoned and never practised again.

The following day, the well-rested newlyweds hosted their very first Drawing Room together. This marked Charlotte's official introduction and, one by one, the courtiers lined up to be presented to her as she stood with her bridesmaids at her side. When the elderly Lord Westmorland saw Lady Sarah Lennox, he dropped to his knees at her feet, mistaking her for the queen. He took her hand, only for the startled Lady Sarah to snatch it back and tell him that he had got the wrong woman. Charlotte took the false start with grace and dignity, showing no flicker of distress. She had no need to, after all, she was married to a man who was already starting to adore her. 'I believe,' wrote bluestocking Elizabeth Montagu shrewdly, 'In vulgar phrase, they will be a happy couple.'[51]

Confined as in a Convent

Unlike some other royal matches, including that of their own eldest son, Charlotte and George seemed to be made for one another. They had similar temperaments, similar interests and a shared distrust of the limelight, and Charlotte had no interest in encouraging the same hotbed of political intrigue that both her predecessor and mother-in-law had stirred up. She was more than happy to obey her husband's instruction to keep out of government business and instead she settled into building a happy home life for herself and the family that the royal couple would raise. Throughout his formative years, George III had been taught by Augusta, George II, and Bute to be suspicious of anyone who seemed to seek his favour. He imparted these same suspicions to his bride, shaping her just as he had been shaped. In the years to come, she came to view the whole world with suspicion, and perhaps we can thank the early years of the marriage for that. Courtier Mrs Harcourt certainly thought that the queen had been ill-served by her husband, who seemed to regard his own cynical view of those around him as the only proper one:

> [George] had been kept locked up till he married & taught to have a bad opinion of the world & almost to dread human honour. That he was therefore delighted with having entirely under his own training a young innocent Girl of 17, for such was the Queen when

she arrived, & that he determined she shd be wholly devoted to him alone, and should have no other friend or society. [The] King on her arrival told her this, & told her that even with the Pss of Wales she was to have as little communication as possible & depend on him & him alone.[52]

It was a risky strategy and, once George fell ill, one that left Charlotte poorly prepared for the challenges that she faced. For now though, the looming threat of the forthcoming Coronation was her only real concern. As Charlotte began to settle in and build a home, it was in the secure knowledge that financially the future was taken care of. Should the king predecease her, Queen Charlotte would receive Somerset House,[53] Richmond Old Park, and an annuity of £100,000, whilst during his lifetime she would receive £40,000 a year from the civil list. For a woman who preferred the hearth to the limelight, it was more than enough to live well.

Though Charlotte's attendant, Juliana Elizabeth von Schwellenberg, known as *Madame*, installed herself as the young queen's closest confidante, it was not *Madame* who would assist her in preparing for the Coronation. Instead, the king called in Henrietta Howard, Countess of Suffolk, the former mistress of George II and Mistress of the Robes to his wife, Caroline. The elderly countess guided the new queen with sympathy through the complicated ceremony that she would face. In an ocean of ambitious courtiers jockeying for position, she was a reassuringly trustworthy pair of hands.

The forthcoming Coronation of King George III whipped the people of London into a frenzy. It had been a long time since they had celebrated the rule of an English monarch, let alone one so young and full of promise, and householders along the Coronation route sold seats in their windows for a small fortune. Many spectators set up camp overnight so they could be sure of getting a good view and the crowds were so deep that fires were banned, in case one got out of hand and caused a catastrophe. By the time dawn broke on 22 September, the newly erected grandstands were full to bursting and soldiers charged with ensuring the crowd behaved were happy to let enterprising spectators push their way to the front in exchange for a few coins. Some even hired out their uniforms, so the more determined royal watchers could get the very best view in the house.

Charlotte, meanwhile, was anything but excited. She was so sick with nerves that she suffered headaches, facial neuralgia, and toothache, but she was determined not to fall prey to the same sort of unfortunate half-dressed calamity that had befallen her at her wedding. Just a fortnight had passed from that day to this, but Charlotte had already learned a thing or two about court life. Mindful that this was George's day, she was absolutely set on making sure that the Coronation went without a hitch. The one thing she did request was that her favourite page, Frederick Albert Papendiek, be sat where she could see him throughout the ceremony. Papendiek's daughter, Charlotte, later entered Queen Charlotte's service as Keeper of the Queen's Wardrobe and reader. Her memoirs offer a fascinating insight into court life.

Though it was another sweltering day, Charlotte once again wore her opulent wedding gown, with a 'Diamond Stomacher, Purple Velvet Sleeves Diamds, Pearls as big as Cherrys, Girdle, Petticoats Diamds, Purple Velvet Surcoat and Mantle with Ermine and Lace, Purple Velvet Cap, only one string of Diamds & Crown Aigrette, Fan Mother of Pearl, Emerald, Rubys and Diamd'.[54] She had received the fan and crown from her husband, and she further enhanced her look with a set of Coronation Locks, better known to us as hair extensions.

As Charlotte processed along the Coronation route beneath a canopy of cloth of gold, Princess Augusta was her chief attendant. Despite appearances, the two women never got along, with Augusta believing her sister-in-law to be a venal and avaricious woman – she wasn't – whilst Charlotte always considered Augusta to be a gossip – she was. Naturally, at the Coronation nobody would have suspected there was anything other than respect between them, and Charlotte looked every inch the composed and regal queen as she swept into Westminster Abbey. This time her clothes stayed put and Charlotte made just the impression she had been hoping for. Perhaps it was a mark of George's affection for his wife that, at the sumptuous Coronation banquet in Westminster Hall that night, he made her the guest of honour.

The hall was packed with the great and the good, all of them sitting in near darkness as they waited for the king and queen to arrive. As soon as Charlotte set foot through the door, a single candle was lit, and its flame travelled along specially prepared flax to illuminate a breath-taking 3,000 wicks all at once. It was a show of pageantry that none would soon forget – least of all the peers who found themselves trying to shelter from the still-smouldering flax as it rained down onto their heads. Few would forget the feast either, a surprisingly meagre repast which gave early warning of the king and queen's preference for the humble over the opulent.

As a young bride, Charlotte's unaffected manner charmed those who encountered her. Shortly after the Coronation, Charlotte and George joined a wealthy Quaker family named Barclay to watch the Lord Mayor's Procession from their opulent mansion. For generations, the Barclay house had been the traditional place from which the monarch viewed the procession and the residents fairly fluttered with excitement at the honour. Though Charlotte was resplendent in diamonds and silver, the daughters of the Quaker family could not have been more different. Their clothes were humble, whilst to their great embarrassment, they found that their French wasn't fluent enough to be able to converse with Charlotte. The queen, however, knew all about being a young lady out of her depth. She asked her attendants to apologise to the girls for the fact that her own English was so poor, and to assure them that she was doing her best to improve it.

Everything seemed to be going splendidly. The king and queen carried out their duties with a smile and were a loving couple behind closed doors, whilst Charlotte welcomed a visit from her beloved brother early in her marriage. Unlike some of his contemporaries, George had no interest in isolating Charlotte from the family that had shaped her, and was happy to welcome them at court. In her spare time, Charlotte studied English with Dr John James Majendie, or played with her dogs, and together the royal couple visited friends, or attempted to. On one occasion, they arrived at Strawberry Hill unannounced, 'and stayed two hours,' wrote Horace Walpole, who lamented that 'I was gone to London but a quarter of an hour before'.[55] To make matters worse, on a previous surprise visit Queen Charlotte had been told that Walpole was still in bed. 'It will certainly be said that I refused to let the Queen see my house,' Walpole sighed. 'Say what it is to have republican servants.'[56] Above all, the royal couple delighted in musical evenings, where Charlotte sang and George accompanied her on the violin. Charlotte's patronage of the arts later led her to commission half a dozen sonatas for the harpsichord from an eight-year-old boy named Wolfgang Amadeus Mozart, who had been recommended by her music tutor, Johann Christian Bach. Those sonatas were *Opus 3*.

But if Charlotte and George were happy, Princess Augusta was not the new queen's only critic. George's mother, Augusta, Dowager Princess of Wales, should have been instrumental in helping her daughter-in-law navigate the ways of court but instead she kept her distance, assessing how much influence Charlotte exercised over the king. Little did Augusta know that George had already warned Charlotte 'never to be alone with [our] mother,' as his brother, Prince William Henry, Duke of Gloucester, told Horace Walpole, 'For she was an artful woman and would try to govern her.' When the king and queen were invited to receive their first public sacrament in St Paul's, Charlotte learned first-hand just how true that was.

All her life, Charlotte had been taught to be humble, a lesson she had promised her mother on her deathbed that she would heed even as queen. It seemed natural, therefore, not to wear her showy jewels to receive the sacrament. She asked George's permission to forgo her jewellery, reminding him that he had removed his crown to receive the sacrament at the Coronation, and he readily agreed. When Charlotte's meddling sister-in-law found out, she took it as a personal slight. Princess Augusta voiced her complaints to her mother, and the Dowager Princess of Wales insisted that George go back on his word and command Charlotte to wear her full regalia at St Paul's. The king backed down and told his wife that she must forget the promise she made to her late mother. Instead, it was his own domineering mother who held sway in the English court. Charlotte obeyed, but she was distraught at having to do so.

Just as George acquiesced to his mother like an obedient little boy, he never really understood the line between looking out for his wife and treating her like a child. Charlotte's youth and lack of ambition were two of the things that most endeared her to the king and he seemed determined to keep her at 17 forever. It left her woefully unprepared for the challenges that the future held.

Charlotte was always at her husband's side when he visited his mother and Lord Bute, but she was never allowed to participate in their meetings. Instead, she was left alone in a room to amuse herself for hours until eventually she asked permission to stay at home instead. Mrs Harcourt was well-placed to witness the comings and goings of life at court and she felt for the queen:

> Coming over with great natural spirits, eagerly expecting to be Queen of a gay Court, finding herself confined as in a convent, & hardly allowed to think without the leave of her husband checked her spirits,

made her fearful & cautious to an extreme, & when
the time came that amusements were allowed her, her
mind was formed to a difft [sic] manner of life.[57]

It was in these early years that the seeds of Charlotte's later years
were planted. Just as her own youthful vivacity was squeezed out
of her in the name of regal propriety, so too did she visit the same
fate on her daughters in the decades to come. For a woman who
had been warned to beware of the domineering Augusta, Charlotte
eventually proved to be more than her match when it came to
exercising control.

But Augusta had nothing to fear from her daughter-in-law.
The Dowager Princess of Wales had become a divisive figure,
suspected of cronyism and nepotism, whilst by contrast Charlotte
was a breath of fresh air for a public jaded by royal wives and
mistresses, some of whom seemed to hold as much sway as
elected officials. Many years after her marriage, when an
ambitious politician used Charlotte's name in his electioneering,
she wrote to Lord Harcourt to disavow him of such notions. 'I am
very much obliged to you,' she wrote, 'For having afforded me
an opportunity of clearing my own character from meddling in
politics, which I abhor equal to sin.'[58]

Charlotte had her passions, but they weren't political. She
loved the theatre, especially the performances of Sarah Siddons,
and tried to get to the opera as often as possible. She took long
strolls through the royal parks and resumed her philanthropic
ways, donating large amounts of money to charities and those in
need, often anonymously. Stories were told in which the queen
plucked a diamond out of her stomacher and gave it to a poverty-
stricken Windsor clergyman, or of her generous gift of two hogs
to a starving family who had allowed the queen and her ladies to
shelter in their cottage from a storm. When their situation had
improved, the householder's grateful wife took a spare-rib all the

way from Windsor to St James's Palace to say thank you. Upon hearing of her exertions, Charlotte gave the woman a meal and yet more gifts by way of gratitude.

Charlotte, who put up the first known English Christmas tree in December 1800, also used the festive period to dispense gifts. She bought the tradition of the Christmas yew branch with her from Germany and put it in pride of place in the Queen's House. As evening fell and the tapers were lit, the court assembled around the yew and sang carols. At Windsor,

> Sixty poor families had a substantial dinner given them … in the middle of the room stood an immense tub with a yew tree placed in it, from the branches of which hung bunches of sweetmeats, almonds and raisins in papers, fruits and toys most tastefully arranged and the whole illuminated by small wax candles. After the company had walked round and admired the tree, each child obtained a portion of the sweets which it bore together with a toy, and then all returned home quite delighted.

Soon the queen's annual philanthropic outgoings had exceeded £5,000. She didn't turn her nose up at so-called fallen women either, and funded housing and educational initiatives for them as well as orphaned young ladies who might be in danger of exploitation. She established funds to care for fifty orphaned daughters of army personnel and fifty of navy personnel, and took a keen interest in their welfare. The queen's patronage was enormously valuable, and institutions such as the Magdalen Hospital flourished under her influence.

Queen Charlotte helped her chosen charities in any way she could, even if it meant enduring yet more public show, and in 1780 she hit on a splendid idea to raise funds. Standing beside a vast birthday cake, the queen greeted debutantes as they were presented to her at the very first occurrence of what was to become known as Queen Charlotte's Ball. With the money raised from the ball, she funded Queen Charlotte's and Chelsea Hospital. The Ball and its traditional birthday cake became an annual event, continuing for decades after the queen's death. Despite its importance in the social calendar, Charlotte wasn't particularly fond of the occasion, as Horace Walpole discovered in 1775.

> The crowd at the Birthday was excessive, and had squeezed, and shoved, and pressed upon the Queen in the most hoyden manner. As she went out of the Drawing-room, somebody said in flattery, 'The crowd was very great.' – 'Yes,' said the Queen, 'and wherever one went, the Queen was in everybody's way.[59]

Yet Charlotte and George weren't entirely without their own extravagances. George gave Charlotte a zebra in 1762 as a belated wedding gift and people came in their hundreds to gaze at the animal as it grazed on the lawns at Buckingham House. Though it may have looked placid, the zebra had a red-hot temper and defied the dreams of naturalists who hoped zebras might be used as carriage animals for the rich. Instead, the queen's pet kicked, bit, and made short work of anybody who tried to tame it. London never would never see domesticated zebras in the streets.

It was in those same streets that Charlotte experienced her first encounter with the vagaries of fame. She was nursing a toothache whilst being carried in her chair through the city, so decided to keep the window closed rather than greet the crowds. The Londoners who pressed close to see her took the slight personally and jeered as she passed by. It was a relief for her to reach home, where she could try to put the unhappy experience out of her mind. Thirty years later, when a stone smashed the glass of her coach and struck Charlotte on the cheek, life had taught her to bear the incident with stoicism.

Behind closed doors, Charlotte and George created a world that was more akin to an upper middle-class household than a royal court. They saved money wherever they could, with the king particularly pleased 'that the Queen will maintain six daughters for less than four were forty nine years ago, when every article of life was cheaper than now.'[60] For a time, all seemed perfect, but the queen would not be able to avoid drama for long.

Act Two

Queen

The Most Deserving of All Friends

Charlotte was everything that George III had wanted, especially because her youth and lack of experience meant that she was just as pliable as he had hoped. When her husband advised her to do something, she did it, and she readily welcomed his decision to personally vet attendees at her Drawing Rooms to ensure that they were suitable company. Memorably described by Frances Burney as 'a peevish old person of uncertain temper and impaired health, swaddled in the buckram of backstairs etiquette', Madame Schwellenberg was happy to help, and tightly controlled access to the young queen to ensure her own influence was never threatened. George and Charlotte were innately suspicious of too much glamour or artfulness, preferring a simple way of life, without even the traditional royal mistresses to muddy the marital waters. An inevitable by-product of this was that Charlotte swiftly began to mimic George's mistrust of anyone who sought his favour. She looked obediently to George for guidance and he was happy to mould her into the wife he had always wanted. As Lord Chesterfield observed, 'She is a good woman, a good wife, a tender mother; and an unmeddling Queen. The King loves her as a woman; but, I verily believe, has never yet spoken one word to her about business.'[1]

As a result, Charlotte never achieved the worldliness that her predecessor or her mother-in-law did. Instead, she tried to stand by her man no matter what, and they spoiled one another rotten. Whilst Charlotte was pregnant with her first child, George acquired Buckingham House for her. She made it into her sanctuary, known to all as the Queen's House. Over the years, this would become the favourite London residence of both the king and queen, where Charlotte liked to relax in her plainly furnished Green Closet. George, himself a keen bookbinder, could often be found whiling away the hours in the impressive library that they created. It was a quiet, contented existence.

They passed the summers at Richmond or Kew, sometimes Windsor, and at each of those residences, the royal family lived in its familiar middle-class way. In all of their houses, Charlotte threw herself into landscaping the gardens, remodelling them and eventually encouraging her daughters to follow her interests in botany, whilst the little princes were given small allotments to tend. Famously, she even created a private menagerie at Kew to house a coterie of exotic beasts.

George and Charlotte shared a dislike for the drab and draughty St James's Palace, and Buckingham House offered everything that that old bastion of royalty did not. Though St James's would remain the official seat of the court, the Queen's House became the home of the family. Indeed, most of the couple's fifteen children were born there, cementing Charlotte and George's love of the place.

It was at the Queen's House that Charlotte arranged an elaborate garden party for her husband's birthday, as she awaited the birth of their first child. Having secured George's promise to stay at St James's for two days, she supervised the installation of an outdoor show at which oiled silk transparencies were used to create a shadow play throughout the grounds. The show opened with a scene in which George III himself held court at a temple of peace, bestowing benevolence on the whole world.

Private parties such as these meant that the king and queen were spared the uncomfortable experience of mixing with the general public, who would be happy to let their rulers know when things weren't going well. Occasionally heckled by the discontented public in the streets or at the theatre, they preferred to stick to private soirees where they could enjoy the company of those who would never dare to voice their dissatisfaction on anything. Charlotte and George liked seclusion, and they cosseted themselves away at every opportunity. It would prove to be a damaging characteristic when it came to the queen's relationships with her children. The first of those children, of which there would eventually be fifteen, came along in 1762.

Charlotte was heavily pregnant when George fell ill with a fever that struck him down without warning. It was a prelude of the trouble to come, and as the queen and her seriously unwell husband passed the summer at Windsor, some began to fear that he might not live, leaving his wife pregnant but the heir, so far, unborn. Happily, George fought off the influenza that threatened to claim his life. By August the couple were back at St James's, with Charlotte's midwife, Mary Draper, standing by.

The slumbering palace was disturbed in the early hours of 12 August 1762, when Queen Charlotte went into labour more than a week beyond her due date. As the hours of Charlotte's suffering passed, her doctor, William Hunter,[2] stood back and wisely let Mrs Draper take the lead. Outside the queen's door, meanwhile, an illustrious party began to gather that included Charlotte's mother-in-law, her maids of honour, the officers of state and some Cabinet members, and, of course, the Archbishop of Canterbury. Of more practical use were Margaret Scott and Elizabeth Chapman, the royal wet nurse and dry nurse respectively, who awaited the call to action.

The night gave way to dawn and still the queen suffered until, just after 7.00 am, Charlotte finally delivered a son. The Tower cannon fired to mark the occasion and the Earl of Huntingdon took to the road to inform the king that he was a father at last. It was regarded as an auspicious omen indeed that, as Charlotte finally rested, a procession made its way through the streets of London carrying a fortune in treasure that had been captured from the Spanish ship, *Hermione*. It travelled directly past St James's Palace but, as the courtiers crowded at the window to get a look at the bounty, Charlotte had eyes only for her little boy.

> Yesterday morning, at twenty-four minutes after seven o'clock, her Majesty was brought to bed of a Prince ...
>
> The Prince is born Duke of Cornwall, and according to custom, will, we suppose, soon be created Prince of Wales, and Earl of Chester.
>
> It is something remarkable, that his Royal Highness was born on the anniversary of his illustrious family's accession to the imperial throne of these kingdoms, and about the hour of the day on which that succession took place.[3]

George Augustus, later to become notorious as the Prince Regent and reign as George IV, was Charlotte's treasure. He slumbered in a cradle of crimson velvet and white satin, decorated with gold lace and an ornate coronet. A vast retinue of staff were entrusted with his care, including two attendants specifically to rock his cradle, and Charlotte and George doted on him. Breaking with accepted protocol, Charlotte even hoped to breastfeed her son, but she was too weak to do so. Eventually, the erstwhile Mrs Scott, mother of a dozen children herself, was called in to perform the service.

Mindful of her duty to produce the heir and the spare, Charlotte was off to a splendid start. Though her labour had not been easy, within a month George wrote to Lord Bute to tell him that Charlotte 'is just up and is thank Heaven very well, and just as nimble as she was a year ago, but very properly keeps sitting that she may not over fatigue herself.'[4] Charlotte had no urgent need to plunge back into her public life, she was simply enjoying being a mother.

As the queen commissioned a life-size wax model of her newborn son, the king lavished her with all the attention she could ask for. He kept her as secluded in England as she had been in her homeland and, with her inner circle vetted for suitability, there was something of the father and daughter in their relationship, despite their numerous children. Charlotte, who had never known any better, felt nothing but loved, but when the king's illness meant that he could no longer be her constant companion, she was ill-equipped to deal with the world in which she found herself.

Over the next three years, Charlotte produced not only a spare in the form of Frederick, Duke of York, but William, Duke of Clarence,[5] too. At home, despite the arrival of the children, little else changed. The king and queen continued to maintain their upper middle-class lifestyle in private, whether at St James's or Kew, Windsor, or Buckingham House, where the family took up residence in summer 1763. The care of their children was overseen by Lady Charlotte Finch, who was to become a royal stalwart, but George and Charlotte were hands-on parents in a way that the previous Georges were not. Both husband and wife had been raised by families in which their parents took an active involvement in the upbringing and education of their children, and they now followed that same example with their own offspring.

Whilst the young royals were subject to a strict educational regime, their parents did not simply hand over responsibility to their governess and tutors. Instead, the king and queen rose daily at 6.00 am and at 8.00 am were joined for breakfast by their elder children, who then went off to their lessons. At 9.00 am, the younger children were brought to their parents for an hour's playtime, and Charlotte visited her children at dinner. Food wasn't extravagant, and Wales in particular rebelled against his plain diet when he was old enough to choose his own menu.

It was Charlotte, too, who insisted that the royal children be variolated against smallpox, and in 1775 she recorded happily that 'my dear Children underwent their operation with all possible and more than expected for heroism.' When she went on to note that, 'I trust that same Providence which has hitherto given me uncommon success in all my undertakings, will not withhold it from me at this time,'[6] Charlotte little knew what tragedies awaited, and how soon they would befall the family.

Whilst George loved to play with the children, chasing them through the palace or crawling on his knees during their games, Charlotte maintained a loving but more reserved approach to parenting. It was she who ensured the children were following their lessons and who interrogated them on what they had learned and how they had improved themselves that day. A letter in the Royal Archives from Princess Augusta finds the 9-year-old girl assuring her mother that 'I am very glad to tell you that I am very good; this morning I behaved Prety [sic] well and this afternoon Quite well'.[7] She went on to let Charlotte know that the other children, in addition to behaving well, joined her in sending their love. Curious to us, but par for the course for Georgian royalty. Yet Charlotte was not without a lighter side, even if on one of the few occasions that she did attempt a more frivolous bit of parenting, it backfired badly.

In 1769, Charlotte thought it would be fun to dress her children up as little statespeople and let them host a Drawing Room to celebrate the anniversary of the king's accession. She hoped that it would be a welcome diversion for her husband, besieged as he was by political headaches.

> The Prince [of Wales] was dressed in scarlet and gold, with the ensigns of the order of the Garter; on his right was the Bishop of Osnaburgh [the Duke of

York] in blue and gold; with the ensigns of the order of the Bath; next to him, on a rich sopha [sic], sat the Princess Royal, with the other Princes to her right, elegantly dressed in Roman togas. The sight of so many fine children, all of one family, their great affability, and the recollection of their dignity, gave the most pleasing impressions to everyone present.[8]

Though the courtiers who attended were charmed – or claimed to be – it was a rare misstep for the queen. She found herself lambasted in the Whig press and by caricaturists for mocking the dignity of the royal family and the ceremonies associated with it. Charlotte never repeated the playful prank and instead concentrated on crafting humble, pious, and sensible adults.

Life wasn't all fun and games, and the royal children were instilled with a strong sense of religious piety, with any wrongdoing severely punished. It was Charlotte who often acted as disciplinarian and her standards were almost unreachably high. One is afforded a glimpse into the expectations she placed on her children by the letter she wrote to the Prince of Wales on his eighth birthday. She told the little boy, 'I recommend unto you the highest love, affection and duty towards the King. Look upon him as a Friend: nay as the greatest, the best and the most deserving of all Friends You can possibly find. Try to imitate his virtues and look upon every thing that is in Opposition to that Duty, as destructive to Yourself.'[9] It was a tall order for a boy still in single digits.

Our Royal Race

By 1765, Charlotte was well settled into her role. She was heavily pregnant with her third son when the king fell ill again, and his mother and Bute descended on the palace, ready to rule the roost.

They assured Charlotte that they had her wellbeing at heart and merely wished to save her from the upset of dealing with George, but they had reckoned without her fierce love for her husband. Suspicious of their influence over him and determined not to abandon George in his hour of need, Charlotte insisted on staying close by his side. As gossip of a power struggle swept through the palace, the Dowager Princess of Wales found her popularity plummeting further than ever.

As the king languished, Madame Schwellenberg pushed Charlotte to confront her mother-in-law and Bute over their behaviour, but this was never in the queen's nature. Instead, she simply remained present, caring for her husband and handling his condition with discretion and love, whilst never directly confronting those who might have sought to exert their influence over him in his weakened state.

Though he made a recovery, external pressures were starting to tell on George's wellbeing. At seemingly constant odds with Parliament and trying to manage both the home front and the deafening sabre-rattling coming from North America, the king and Parliament alike began to consider a Regency Bill, which would be implemented should a monarch ever be too unwell to rule. Tellingly, fears of how George's mother might try to exploit this to her own ends were a major topic of debate. Whoever the Regent might be, should there ever be a Regent at all, it was unlikely to be the Dowager Princess of Wales. Instead, it was decided that the ideal candidate would be Charlotte, the last person on earth who wanted the job.

There were domestic dramas breaking out, too. Madame Schwellenberg's hard-line approach towards the Dowager Princess of Wales had angered George's mother to the point that she demanded Charlotte dismiss her confidante. Augusta blamed Madame Schwellenberg for rumours that she and Bute had attempted to manipulate the king's illness in their own favour, and gossip was rife that Augusta had flatly refused to let her son leave London, despite the air out of town being much better for his convalescence. All of this, coupled with Augusta's attempts to control the dissemination of news about the king's health not only to the public, but to his family too, combined to shake Charlotte's nerves.

It was this that caused Madame Schwellenberg to encourage Charlotte to stand up to her mother-in-law once and for all. Though Charlotte chose the path of least resistance and concentrated on George instead, word of Madame's criticisms got back to Augusta. As George recovered, his mother demanded that he send Madame back to Germany and, for a time, he seriously considered doing so. If he had gone through with the plan, it would have sent a clear message about which woman was truly the king's favourite, but he relented in the face of Charlotte's distressed pleas. Instead, he contented himself with dressing down Madame in front of his wife. Charlotte might have won the battle, but she had felt the glancing blow of Augusta's ire in doing so.

Though Charlotte felt the slight on behalf of her trusted confidante, she remained her husband's greatest champion. Already contending with domestic political troubles and with the American War of Independence on the horizon, he needed it. Life became a curious cocktail of happiness and misery, and the births of Charlotte, Princess Royal, followed by Edward, Duke of Kent and Strathearn, and Princess Augusta Sophia, were punctuated by the deaths of George's 28-year-old brother Edward, Duke of York, in 1767 and his sister, Louisa, the following year. The couple were particularly happy to welcome another daughter, who would be a playmate for the little Princess Royal, but good news was to be in short supply.

And for the king and queen, the dramas just kept on coming. In 1769, George's brother, Prince Henry, Duke of Cumberland and Strathearn, was successfully sued for adultery by Lord Grosvenor. The name of the royal family was dragged through the mud as every detail of the embarrassing scandal was picked apart. It was a mortifying experience for George and Charlotte but two years later, when Cumberland confessed to having married a widowed commoner named Mrs Anne Horton, the king reached his limit. He banished Cumberland, a fate that awaited another brother, Prince William Henry, Duke of Gloucester and Edinburgh, when he confessed to a clandestine marriage to commoner Maria Walpole. With both brothers banished from court, an increasingly embattled George pushed the Royal Marriages Act of 1772 through Parliament, forbidding any marriage without the express consent of monarch and Parliament, except in exceptional circumstances.

This was an Act that Charlotte, with her devotion to piety and faithfulness, and her belief in the superiority of royal blood, wholeheartedly supported. Morality and religious faith went hand in hand, and Charlotte had no qualms about rejecting those she considered unsuitable. The infamous Emma Hamilton, for instance, was never received at court due to a personal ban by Queen Charlotte. As the Persian ambassador, Mirza Abul Hassan Khan, noted, 'no member of a family touched by scandal is received at court'. George's own brothers would not be welcomed back until 1780, when Charlotte noted in a letter to Prince William, 'The report of the King's being reconciled to his Brothers is true. It seems to give universal satisfaction in public, but makes no difference in our way of living at Windsor.'[10]

Queen Charlotte encouraged her husband's fears of a world in which Cumberland's marriage catapulted the kingdom into something like the Wars of the Roses, pitting brother against brother and forcing the people of England to choose their side. The sanctity of royal marriage and royal blood was close to Charlotte's heart, and she wasn't above reminding her husband that his own great-grandmother, Sophia Dorothea of Celle, had a commoner for a mother. The queen even upbraided her husband about the matter at a dinner with Lord Dover at Frogmore, crowing about her own pure royal origins, versus those of her husband. Charlotte 'derived such pleasure even from trifles,' wrote Lord Dover, '[but] we are also glad that our royal race should possess this mixture of lower, but not therefore worst blood, which separates them from the pedigree-hunting princes of the empire.'[11]

Queen Charlotte was devoted to her duty and her family, but she was equally devoted to protocol, and she expected everybody else to follow suit. Charlotte insisted on full formal court dress, sticking rigidly to her decision even when fashions changed. She wouldn't countenance the fashion for tall feathers in the hair, and the more on-trend courtiers delighted in seeing just how far they could push her. Yet when the Duchess of Devonshire appeared in feathers so tall that she could barely fit through the door, Charlotte kept her counsel. Likewise, when the Duchess of Hamilton's tardiness caused the queen to be late for a play, Charlotte didn't rebuke her. Instead, she killed with kindness, presenting the Duchess with a diamond-studded watch, so that she would never be late again.

Courtiers sometimes struggled with elaborate court gowns, and could not sit in the royal presence without permission. On some occasions, they could only move when instructed to do so, even missing meals and ending the day hungry and exhausted. Queen Caroline, wife of George II, had always been happy to let the highest ranked courtier present serve as her aide, but Queen Charlotte would do no such thing. At her court, rank in the peerage came second to the rank of office held in the royal household, and all were expected to remember it.

Charlotte adhered to the rule that no man but the king himself could sit in her presence, and even the highest ranked male visitors were never served refreshments if the queen were present without her husband. Even her own sons dined at her attendants' tables if they were required to eat, since there was no other place for them to sit. Charlotte would make no exceptions, though. Protocol was protocol.

Not all queens were so proper. In 1772, George's sister Caroline Matilda, Queen of Denmark, was revealed to have been having an affair with Johann Friedreich Struensee, the doctor of her mentally unstable husband. Struensee and Caroline Matilda ruled Denmark as unofficial regents whilst the king occupied himself in the brothels of Copenhagen, but a coup by his stepmother brought the house of cards tumbling down. The result was the execution of Struensee and the divorce and house arrest of Caroline Matilda, who died in 1775 at the age of 23. Caroline Matilda had begged her brother, George III, to let her come home to England, but he wouldn't countenance such a thought. Although the affair was mostly kept out of the papers, the strain at home was enormous.

Charlotte, of course, had a family of her own back in Mecklenburg, and she took a keen interest in their business. Her sister had been prevented from pursuing her own chance of happiness with the Duke of Roxburghe, but her brother and the heir to the dukedom, Prince Charles, had made a happy marriage to Princess Frederica of Hesse-Darmstadt. Though the groom was eleven years older than his wife, Charles and Frederica got on famously and were soon parents. Such cheerful news was followed by a short visit by Charles to England, where he and Charlotte enjoyed a joyful reunion. When she said a tearful goodbye, she could hardly guess how much worse things were about to get.

Charlotte managed the household and approved the educational programme of her daughters as well, personally appointing the members of the nursery team. It was a duty she took very seriously indeed. Her right-hand woman was Lady Charlotte Finch, who the queen usually left to her own devices. When she stepped outside her remit though, even this long-time and fiercely loyal retainer wasn't above a telling off.

When a member of Lady Charlotte's team was relieved of her duties amid allegations of alcoholism, it was Lady Charlotte herself who had to issue the bad news. Yet when Lady Charlotte attempted to make a recommendation as to who should replace her, the queen was quick to tell her to mind her manners. Lady Charlotte had the temerity to bring her complaints in person to her employer, who replied in a letter in which she politely but firmly put her in her place.

'You said that in coming into the Family you felt some distress in not having appointed the subgoverness,' wrote Charlotte. 'This place is not to be disposed of by either the Governor or Governess but by us alone, their recommendations are taken as well and in preference to others, but the choice and determination lies solely in us.'[12] She did graciously agree that Lady Charlotte, who was in attendance for a minimum of six hours during the daytime and as late into the evening as the queen dictated, could have two days off each week. In agreeing to this, however, Charlotte told her that 'I must beg of you that the other days you will rather increase your own attendance upon the Children.' Queen Charlotte was a hard taskmaster, but she knew the value of having such a trusted retainer in charge of her offspring. In fact, 'the real good of my Children has made me speak I am sorry that myself have not more time to spend with them,' she told Lady Charlotte, 'and therefore am thankful to Providence for having worthy people about them.'[13] Few were more worthy than Lady Charlotte Finch.

In 1775, Buckingham House was transferred to Queen Charlotte as her dower house by an Act of Parliament, in exchange for Somerset House, traditionally the dower house of her predecessors. As the Buckingham and Somerset House exchange was being completed, Charlotte's ladies-in-waiting were causing her headaches at home. They complained that the queen kept them so busy that they had no time to eat the free, if meagre, supper that was their right. They were further put out when Charlotte's adherence to court protocol meant that they were forbidden from styling themselves in the most modern way, especially after she had banned them from wearing long feathers in their hair. The queen left it up to her husband to negotiate with her ladies and he took the path of least resistance, offering each of them a payment of £70 and the promise that they would not go hungry again. Though the matter of the feathers was never resolved, Charlotte grudgingly agreed that she would make a gift of £1,000 to each of her attendants on the occasion of their marriage. To a woman, they accepted.

The Late Dowager

> This morning between the hours of six and seven, her Royal Highness the Princess Dowager of Wales departed this life to the great grief of their Majesties and all the Royal Family, after a very long and painful illness, which she bore with the greatest fortitude and resignation.[14]

From the day of her marriage, Charlotte had been regarded by Augusta, Dowager Princess of Wales, as a threat. The two women had never formed a close bond and Augusta even installed her attendant, Miss Dashwood, in Charlotte's household as a spy. Not that there was much worth spying on. Far from political or personal intrigue, Charlotte in private was little different to Charlotte in public. Augusta took nothing for granted, though, and even as she battled terminal throat cancer, she was determined to keep control.

For all her fierce determination to survive, Augusta was nearing the end. By now married and living overseas, Augusta, Duchess of Brunswick, returned to nurse her dying mother. She and Charlotte had never got along and now, eight years since Princess Augusta had left England for Brunswick, relations had not thawed. Augusta's return to nurse her namesake mother was a public relations success, even if Charlotte was far from happy to see her. Though the family gave every impression of a united front, this time the queen was determined not to be undermined and pushed out by her sister-in-law. When Charlotte's brother visited England, he had been given apartments at St James's, but Augusta was tucked away on Pall Mall, a sure sign that she was not welcome. The queen made sure her foe had no opportunity to spend time alone with George, and when she and Augusta were forced to spend time together, Charlotte treated her with cool civility.

Eventually things reached a head when a spat broke out at a ball in honour of the queen's official birthday,[15] which the Duchess of Brunswick attended in the company of her friend and former Woman of the Bedchamber, Lady Gower. When the ladies made their way into the ballroom, the Duchess of Argyll, Charlotte's attendant, allowed Lady Gower to go ahead of her so she could sit beside Augusta. The following day, the furious queen upbraided the duchess in front of her household, telling her that 'The Princess of Brunswick has nothing to do here!' What had been unthinkable just a decade earlier was now a reality: Charlotte no longer needed anybody's guidance to navigate court.

The Dowager Princess of Wales died on 8 February 1772. The following day, her daughter, Lady Augusta, packed her belongings and prepared to return to her marital home in protest at her treatment at Charlotte's hands. Though she was convinced to remain a little longer and observe mourning, few members of the public mourned with her. The funeral of Augusta of Saxe-Gotha was marked by public unrest. Her coffin was spat at and 'the mob huzzaed for joy'[16] as the mourning cloth was torn down at Westminster Abbey. It seemed as though all of England, from the people to the palace, was in upheaval, but Augusta's death brought with it the end of the quiet war for supremacy. From now on, there would be only one woman in charge of the royal household.

Kew Palace had been Augusta's favourite residence and, following her death, the royal family adopted it as their summer home. Kew replaced Richmond Lodge as the place in which they could escape the bustle of London, and the king immediately commissioned a series of renovations to the White House, to make it more suitable for his ever-expanding family. The elder princes were given a residence at Kew's Dutch House, whilst the younger boys, William and Edward, were housed in Cambridge Cottage, leaving infant Ernest and princesses Charlotte, Augusta, and Elizabeth with their parents.

Yet whilst the family was growing, the eldest of the royal children was becoming a thorn in the side of his parents. The Prince of Wales was a pleasure-seeker extraordinaire, who loved nothing more than the company of rogues and ladies of dubious repute, and spent his days gambling and spending. He thought nothing of touching his parents for bailouts and never learned anything approaching a lesson. Eventually Charlotte sought an audience with her oldest son, and his report of it to his favourite brother, the Duke of York, leaves no room for doubt on how the conversation had gone.

> I am sorry to tell you yt. ye unkind behaviour of both their Majesties, but in particular of the Queen, is such yt. it is hardly bearable. She and I, under the protestations of ye. greatest friendship, had a long conversation together. She accused me of various high crimes and misdemeanours, all wh. I answered, & in ye vulgar English phraze [sic] gave her as good as she brought. She spoke to me, she said, entirely without ye King's knowledge. Now I am thoroughly convinced from ye language she used & ye style she spoke in she must previously have talked ye subject over with ye King, who wanted to try whether I could

be intimidated or not, but when she found I was not so easily to be intimidated, she was silent; after having tried various topicks [sic] in order to vex me, finding yt. yt. was a very difficult task, she eventually began talking about us both, & abused you monstrously, as well as me.[17]

With her son causing trouble in town, Charlotte threw herself into life at Kew and the opportunity to indulge her lifelong love of botany, just as George indulged his own passion for tilling the land. At Kew, she redesigned the gardens with Capability Brown, adding a thatched cottage in which she hosted afternoon tea and which was later beautifully decorated by her daughter, Princess Elizabeth. She famously kept a menagerie which was filled with exotic birds and beasts, some of which were gifts from her son, William, when he was serving overseas. She wrote to him in 1782 to thank him for 'The Dear [sic] [which] is so so beautiful & Tame that it eat [sic] Bread out of my Hand when it arrived. The birds seem hitherto to do well in this Climate and I intend visiting them [at Richmond] very soon.'[18]

Also among Charlotte's exotic pets were the first ever kangaroos to arrive in the United Kingdom. These kangaroos proved to be so fecund that their offspring were offered as gifts to courtiers, to prevent them from entirely taking over the grounds at Kew. The children played merrily on the manicured lawns and each week the public were admitted to the gardens to catch a glimpse of the king and queen, who would often make a point of coming to the window to greet their subjects. Charlotte soon extended her beneficence to her neighbours too, and met a good many of them during her walks in the village. Wherever she went, it seemed that good deeds followed.

In 1776, with the colonies agitating for their independence and war raging in North America, the king sought to find a sanctuary from his woes. George took ownership of the Queen's Garden Lodge at Windsor, which he renovated at an enormous cost to create the Queen's Lodge.[19] This became one of the couple's favourite residences, with their daughters safely billeted in Lower Lodge under the watchful eye of Lady Charlotte Finch. 'Windsor is just the thing for us,' said a contented Charlotte, as she settled into a new routine at this welcome sanctuary. Their London home was the Queen's House, whilst in the summer they split their time equally between Kew, for official or social engagements, or Windsor, when they wished for privacy. Holidays were taken on the coast, and so the routine went on year after year. This was the very model of the quiet and secluded life that the king and queen both relished. It was also the polar opposite of the scandalous, wild life that the young Prince of Wales was determined to lead, much to the horror of his parents.

A dozen years of near constant pregnancy had taken their toll on Charlotte, and her youthful enthusiasm had morphed into an agreeable, if insular nature. It would later give way to anxiety and a red-hot temper, but Charlotte was not without provocation. The events of the next few years would have proved challenging to anyone's temperament.

A Certain Want of Something

Through death, divorce, scandal, and war, Charlotte stood solidly by George. The family continued to grow until, by 1780, it numbered fourteen children. The last sons to be born to the couple – though there would still be one more daughter – were Octavius in 1779 and Alfred in 1780. Riots in London left the king exhausted and, more than ever, he and Charlotte looked to their youngest children for comfort. The Prince of Wales was making waves in the gossip columns thanks to a tumultuous private life and York and Clarence were gone, the former to a military education in Germany, and the latter to sea and a career in the navy. Despite this, the routine at home had barely changed at all, though George was at his desk more than ever before.

The Prince of Wales had embarked on adulthood with gusto. Finding his dreams of joining the army were denied him by the king, he threw himself instead into politics and partying. Whilst his father was a loyal Tory, Wales allied himself with the Whig opposition, incurring his mother's disapproval for doing so. Yet with George mostly opting to maintain a dignified silence on the matter, Charlotte had no choice but to do likewise.

Charlotte found the pregnancies that produced Octavius and Alfred the most difficult of all. She was exhausted by nearly twenty years of bearing children, and it should come as no surprise that Amelia, who was born in 1783, was the last entrant to the royal nursery. She was the final member of what her mother called the 'amiable graces', but before she was born, the royal family was to face a double tragedy.

The smallpox variolation of the youngest children seemed to be a matter of routine, just as it had been in the past. This time, however, tragedy struck, and Little Alfred, who was eighteen years younger than his oldest brother, fell ill soon after receiving the treatment. Lady Charlotte Finch took him off to Deal, where it was believed that the sea air would soon see him rally. At first he seemed to improve, and Charlotte wrote with obvious relief and joy to Lady Charlotte Finch, in answer to a heartening report of the little prince's health.

> There is so much Comfort in all Your accounts from Deal Castle that I cannot possibly deprive myself any longer the pleasure of expressing my joy upon it. May it please Providence to restore Your little charge to his Natural Health and Spirits that We may the sooner have the pleasure of seeing You amongst us again.[20]

Instead of recovering, Alfred's condition grew steadily worse. He broke out in smallpox-like blemishes and, struggling to breathe, was brought back to Windsor Castle and the care of his loving parents. Alfred languished for six weeks as the nation followed his sad decline in regular newspaper updates, which alternated between suggestions that he was on the road to recovery and hints that there was no hope for his survival. Alfred died on 20 August 1782, leaving Charlotte inconsolable. To Lady Charlotte Finch, she sent a lock of hair that had belonged to 'my dear little Angel Alfred', and asked her to wear it 'not only in remembrance of that dear Object, but also as a mark of esteem from Your Affectionate Queen.'[21] Days later, Charlotte wrote to her son, William, seeking some solace.

> [Alfred's] strength decreased Daily, and this dear little suffering object dyed [sic] the 20th of August about five a clock in the Evening. This event though foreseen was a very trying one for the king, myself and every Body about us ... this little Angel now is far happier ... yet must I own my weakness, that I do feel a certain want of something which I cannot find. Providence has been uncommonly Gracious to me in every Respect and particularly in that of preserving me a large Family and even in this Stroke He was singularly Gracious, for it was the Youngest and least known of my children He deprived me of.[22]

Alfred was the first of Charlotte's children to die, and she clung to Octavius as she grieved for her little boy. The king, meanwhile, admitted that though he was devastated by the loss of Alfred, had it been Octavius who had died, then he would wish to join him.

Charlotte was pregnant with Amelia when Octavius was variolated against smallpox and, to the horror of the family, he too fell ill.

Although Alfred's decline had been slow, Octavius's was anything but, leaving precious little time to say goodbye. He died at Kew on 3 May 1783, plunging his father into a depression from which he never fully recovered, and which only deepened with the constant bad news from North America. As she so often did when faced with the unthinkable, the queen took solace in the Lord. Once again, she faced the task of letting William know that his brother was dead. The queen's grief and fortitude are evident from one of the letters that she wrote to her son, when she prayed, 'may it please the Almighty to preserve those that remain, and that they may prove to be Good Christians and useful Members of Society, this is the greatest Ambition, and I hope that this my wish will not fail to be fulfilled.'[23]

It was a grieving family that greeted the birth of little Princess Amelia just three months later. Celebrations were muted this time.

Some Secret Terror

With the deaths of Alfred and Octavius, something changed in the royal household. It was a subtle but permanent shift that began the start of the melancholic affliction that would come to blight the family in the years to come. The household was shaken by a mysterious illness that seized Princess Elizabeth in 1786, striking the vivacious girl down in one fell swoop. As Elizabeth was blistered and bled, her siblings developed whooping cough and the spectre of the two dead princes loomed large in everyone's mind.

Though Elizabeth recovered, her painfully drawn-out convalescence was one more plank in the worries of the king and queen. When Margaret Nicholson made an attempt on George's life in 1786, it seemed as though all the cares in the world were assailing them. Claiming that she wished to present a petition, Nicholson lunged at the king as he climbed down from his carriage at St James's. She lashed out at him with a blunt dessert knife but was easily restrained by guards. George correctly intuited that Nicholson posed no real threat and told the guards that 'the poor creature is mad; do not hurt her, she has not hurt me.' Nicholson, it transpired, had been driven to insanity when she was deserted by a lover and left destitute. She believed herself to be the rightful heir to the throne and admitted that she had no wish to kill the king, merely to frighten him. As punishment, she was committed to Bedlam, where she remained until her death four decades later.

The queen wasn't present when Nicholson attacked George, and he immediately departed for Windsor to be sure that she didn't hear the report second-hand. Though George played down the incident once he arrived there, Charlotte's attendants broke into dramatic weeping when they heard what had happened. Charlotte, however, was rather more composed. 'I envy you,' she told the ladies, 'For I cannot cry.' Charlotte was badly shaken, but things were only going to get worse.

Laid low by grief, battling his eldest son's excesses, and embattled by conflicts of all kinds, in 1788 George III was struck down by terrible stomach pains that his doctors blamed on stress. Although Charlotte had successfully weathered the earlier storms of the prospective Regency Bill, her respite was to be a temporary one and, in 1788, life for the royal couple changed forever. Shattered by political feuding, conflict overseas and grief, the king was in dire straits. Business detained him in London through the early summer until, by the time Parliament rose, he was desperate to escape the capital.

Lord Fauconberg, one of the king's Lords of the Bedchamber, was a great exponent of the health benefits of a trip to Cheltenham Spa and George was keen to try it out. Encouraged by his physician, Sir George Baker, the king decided that he and Charlotte, along with their three eldest daughters, would spend the summer at Cheltenham. It was their first trip to the English countryside and since Cheltenham was still fairly humble – though the royal visit would change all that – they would stay at Lord Fauconberg's home.

Though George had faced a critical public in London, the further he got from the capital, the more happy his subjects were to see him. The six blissful weeks the family spent in Cheltenham seemed to do wonders for George's constitution. Each morning, he and Charlotte breakfasted together before taking a trip or visiting friends, whilst each evening they strolled through town, merrily greeting the public who came out to see them. By the time the summer reached an end and the family set out for Kew, the king's anxieties seemed to have completely vanished.

The family had scarcely arrived at Kew before it became evident that things were not well. The king's attendants became concerned at his changeable moods, by turns irritable and angry or overly affectionate, and he complained of mysterious pains. All of this sounded worryingly familiar to Charlotte from his brief illness of 1765 and she hungrily gathered every scrap of intelligence about her husband's condition from his attendants, trying to fathom just how bad things might get. The family were due to relocate to Windsor, but Charlotte was concerned that George wasn't well enough to do so. This seemed to be confirmed when the king summoned his physician, Sir George Baker, and complained that he was suffering from agonising stomach pains. Charlotte asked Baker to advise the king not to travel, but George was determined to attend an official engagement at St James's. Though he managed to endure the event, George was clearly unwell and immediately made for the Queen's Lodge at Windsor once he had finished his duties.

The trip to Windsor would prove fateful, for as soon as he was greeted by the queen and the four youngest princesses, George fell into hysterics. When a similar incident occurred during a church service the following day, Charlotte sent for Baker. Though Charlotte hoped to speak to the doctor alone, George refused to be parted from her, despite Baker's entreaties that he should rest. Yet rest was one thing that George could not do. The stomach pains returned, so severe this time that the queen dashed from his apartments 'in great alarm, in her *shift*, or with very little clothes', and urgently begged his pages to summon David Dundas, the king's surgeon. These pains, accompanied by agonising cramps in his legs and an angry red rash, heralded the start of a prolonged period of mental and physical illness. It would not be the last, nor the most severe.

Soon George was feverish and barely slept; when he spoke, it was in rambling sentences and as the weeks brought no change, Charlotte's heart and spirits plummeted. She sought solace in the Bible, and assured her husband that God would not impose any suffering without the knowledge that they could not overcome it. Hearing those words, the king embraced her and said, 'then you are prepared for the worst.'

Despite George's pronouncements, Charlotte was anything but prepared. Though she tried to hide her anxiety from her husband, when she was alone with her attendants, she broke down. To make matters worse, George seemed to recover and decline constantly, raising and dashing his family's hopes until Charlotte was beside herself. He still refused to cancel any of his engagements and returned to London when his duties required it, where his dishevelled appearance caused his ministers to take him aside and help him tidy his clothing.

'The Queen is almost overpowered with some secret terror,' wrote Frances Burney who, as Queen Charlotte's co-Keeper of the Robes with Juliana Elizabeth von Schwellenberg, was privy to her most private and unguarded moments.

> I am affected beyond all expression in her presence, to see what struggles she makes to support serenity. To-day she gave up the conflict when I was alone

with her, and burst into a violent fit of tears. It was very, very terrible to see! … Sometimes she walks up and down the room without uttering a word, but shaking her head frequently, and in evident distress and irresolution.[24]

Powerless to help her husband, Charlotte felt even more helpless when the Prince of Wales sent his own physician, Richard Warren, to give a second opinion on the king. With father and son on opposing sides of the political divide and Warren a close confidante of the Whig glitterati, Charlotte suspected a conspiracy to have George declared unfit to rule and Wales installed as Regent. If that happened, the queen would be entirely at the mercy of the Prince of Wales too. She would not be a widow, entitled to her annuity and dower, but the wife of a man who might yet live for decades.

Charlotte agreed to let Warren speak to her husband but asked that she be informed of his findings. When she saw from the window that the physician was instead leaving the lodge and heading for the castle, the residence of the Prince of Wales, she was beside herself. For the first time, Charlotte had tangible proof that the prince was pulling the strings. Believing herself powerless, Charlotte let her anguish and frustration out in other ways. When the *Morning Herald* reported that the king was believed to be unwell, she was apoplectic. She hurled the paper into a fire and demanded that the printer be brought to book. Just a few days later, a shocking occurrence at the family dinner table left such petty concerns forgotten.

By now, the once healthy monarch with a love of working the land was a shadow of the man he had been. His swollen legs were swathed in bandages and his eyes bulged from a shaven skull. He leaned heavily on a walking stick and talked incessantly for the duration of the meal, barely pausing to eat. If that wasn't bad enough, as dinner reached its conclusion, he suddenly rose from his chair, seized the Prince of Wales by the throat, and flung him across the room. Charlotte gathered up her daughters and fled for the safety of her locked room, where she spent the night in tearful prayers.

As Charlotte tried to sleep in the room she shared with George, he marched up and down the floor, talking constantly. Eventually, she had no choice but to have him removed, and the king was placated with a bed next door in Charlotte's dressing room, where he was attended by equerries throughout the night to keep him from bursting in on her. Even then, she barely slept and instead paced the floor into the early hours, tormented by her husband's suffering and the ambition of his heir.

Frances Burney tended the queen in the days after the incident at the dinner table and recalled that her mistress's spirits seemed to plummet from that moment on. In fact, during the first night on which the king and his equerries were billeted in the dressing room, Burney visited Charlotte and found her health had taken a turn for the worse.

> My poor Royal mistress! Never can I forget her countenance – pale, ghastly pale she looked; she was seated to be undressed, and attended by lady Elizabeth Waldegrave and Miss Goldsworthy; her whole frame was disordered, yet she was still and quiet.[25]

The following morning, things had not improved. As the whole household quaked with imagined horrors at the condition of the king, it was Miss Burney who tended to the ailing queen.

> O what horror in every face I met! ... She looked like death – colourless and wan; but nature is infectious; the tears gushed from her own eyes, and a perfect agony of weeping ensued, which, once begun, she could not stop; she did not, indeed, try; for when it

subsided, and she wiped her eyes, she said, 'I thank you, Miss Burney – you have made me cry – it is a great relief to me – I had not been able to cry before, all this night long.'[26]

And what a night it had been. Miss Burney learned that in the deepest hours of the night, the king had become convinced that his wife had been smuggled out of the house and would not rest until he saw her himself. He dashed into her room, pulled back the bedcurtains, and gazed at Charlotte by candlelight for half an hour, unspeaking. 'The depth of terror during that time no words can paint,'[27] said Miss Burney, but the impact on the queen was devastating. She became terrified of another evening invasion and eventually began to lock her door to keep her husband out.

The year 1788 was one of crisis for Charlotte and she came to rely on her ladies more than ever, yet they could only watch helplessly as she refused to eat, or set aside her food to pray. Fearful that her despair was somehow contagious, she would only see her children for short periods, and the atmosphere grew steadily more oppressive. When an ever-growing legion of physicians arrived to give their learned opinions on the monarch, Charlotte grew more and more hysterical each time George refused to see them. Those who did gain admittance reported not to the queen, but left her in the dark, and gave the Prince of Wales their verdicts instead. It was a bitter blow. The one thing they all agreed on was that the king should be removed from the dressing room, as seeing Charlotte only seemed to make his behaviour worse. With an anguished cry of 'What will become of me!' the queen consented. Only now did she agree to receive her daughters. That night, the princesses and their mother wept together for the fate of the family.

Warren was of the opinion that the monarch would only recover if he was kept under strictly controlled conditions. With her husband shut away, the queen became likewise isolated, locking herself into her chambers until whispers began to spread that the king might be on his deathbed. Warren decided that George's access to his family should be restricted until it was virtually zero, allowing them only to walk past his window at a distance. When George saw them, he became frantic, hammering on the glass and crying out until the terrified youngest girls turned tail and ran.

How different the world was from the scene described by Frances Burney just a few years earlier, when she witnessed a scene of domestic harmony that even more than two decades of married life hadn't dimmed:

> The Queen had nobody but myself with her, one morning, when the King hastily entered the room, with some letters in his hand, and addressing her in German, which he spoke very fast, and with much apparent interest in what he said, he brought the letters up to her, and put them into her hand. She received them with much agitation, but evidently of a much pleased sort, and endeavoured to kiss his hand as he held them. He would not let her, but made an effort, with a countenance of the highest satisfaction, to kiss hers. I saw instantly in her eyes a forgetfulness at the moment, that any one was present, while drawing away her hand, she presented him her cheek. He accepted her kindness with the same frank affection that she offered it; and the next moment they both spoke English and talked upon common and general subjects.
>
> What they said I am far enough from knowing; but the whole was too rapid to give me time to quit the room; and I could not but see with pleasure that the Queen had received some favour with which she was sensibly delighted, and that the King, in her acknowledgments, was happily and amply paid.[28]

On the day that she and George were separated, the Prince of Wales and the Duke of York begged an audience with their mother. Her attendants feared that more trouble might be on the way, but instead they behaved with the utmost respect. They spent the day with their mother and sisters in private, and when the princes left that evening, the queen seemed to have rallied a little. She even agreed to use a different suite of rooms for now, so that her husband wouldn't be able to appear unexpectedly even if he wanted to.

The Queen is Really King

Sir George Baker, eminent and respected physician that he was, could not help the king, and a king whose mania was out of control could not serve his country. He couldn't even make a speech to declare the State Opening of Parliament, meaning that even though the need to discuss a Regency was more urgent than ever, Parliament could not convene to hold such discussions. Despite this, politicians began to consider the matter of the Regency anyway, and the most important question was who should take the reins.

Though Wales's womanising and spending had already caused headaches for his parents, in particular an embarrassingly public dalliance with the actress Mary Robinson, he had never seemed to hunger for power. The queen herself loathed her son's attachment to Mary Robinson and had once requested that she remove herself from a theatrical box in order to save the family's embarrassment. When Mary refused to go, she must have felt like the queen-in-waiting, but her fleeting relationship with the prince left her ruined. By the time the king's health failed and his ravings were bordering on violent, Mary was nothing but one in a lengthening line of the prince's failed relationships. Yet when serious debate began about who should rule if the king was unable to do so, it was that same gadabout prince who was the prime candidate. Though earlier proposals for a Regency Bill had been forestalled by George's return to health, this time there didn't appear to be much hope for a miracle cure.

When discussion of the apparently inevitable Regency reached the Parliamentary debating chamber, there seemed to be only one answer as to who would serve. The Whigs argued that the only suitable candidate was the heir to the throne himself, and it did no harm that the Prince of Wales happened to be a committed and passionate Whig. Wales attempted to keep out of the fray, but when he visited his father, he found a suspicious Charlotte waiting. She was convinced that he and York had been conspiring with Wales's close friend, the Whig leader Charles James Fox, to seize the reins of power and line his own pockets. William Pitt the Younger, of course, was the man who would navigate the potential bill through Parliament. As leader of the Tories, he was no friend of Fox.

Perhaps mindful that Wales could end up as Prince Regent, Pitt crafted a bill that would put tight curbs on the power of the Regent, whoever that might be. It also guaranteed that the Regent would have no power over the king's care and household, a responsibility that would remain wholly in the hands of his wife. Whilst Charlotte was motivated not by politics, but by loyalty and love to her husband, this wasn't how her opponents interpreted it. To them, it was a sure sign that she intended to keep the king on a tight leash and the Prince of Wales was badly piqued by the fact that he wouldn't get his hands on his father's worldly goods. With his debts climbing ever higher, they would have provided him with quite a payday. Charlotte feared that letting him have free rein over the royal estates might prove financially catastrophic, and she dreaded the damage that could be done if he took power, ejected the Tories – ever loyal to the monarch – and installed the Whigs in their place.

Yet whilst Wales was certainly ambitious, such conspiracy theories owed more to Charlotte's frantic fears than reality. She was at her wits' end and desperate to lash out. Wales provided a handy – and often insensitive – target for her anger. *The Times*, meanwhile, put a more balanced view, though the truth for the Prince of Wales was somewhere in the middle:

> The PRINCE has conducted himself since the indisposition of his father with great propriety – Those who call themselves his party, have said much more than they were ever warranted to pronounce, by either his commands or his surmizes [sic]; so that they have done his Royal Highness a disadvantage on the occasion.[29]

Whilst Charlotte was feuding with her eldest sons, she began to put in place the foundations of what would become known as 'the Windsor nunnery'. She gathered her six daughters to her as secretaries, confidantes, and friends, and as the years passed, proved highly resistant to letting them go. Charlotte's reliance on George to shape her world would lead to her shaping the worlds of almost all of her daughters too.

Despite her fears, Charlotte still prayed that George would recover and render the Regency Bill unnecessary. Just in case he didn't, she was happy to put all her faith in Pitt and the Tories. Of course, not everyone saw it this way and it was inevitable that some would speculate 'whether [George] or the Queen is really King'.[30] Only time would tell.

Where the King Is, There Shall I Be

As debate raged in Parliament over the Regency Bill, at Windsor, Charlotte grew ever more wretched. A procession of physicians was marched through the sovereign's chambers in an effort to find a cure for his condition, but only one seemed to hold out much hope. With their expertise seemingly failing them, the royal physicians decided that they should move the king to Kew, where he would benefit from the fresh country air. Charlotte, however, was not so sure. She confided in Lady Harcourt her belief that Wales hoped to keep her from her husband, the better to seize power, and she firmly believed that if George was taken to Kew, then Wales would do all he could to prevent her from following.

The move could not happen without Charlotte's permission, which she was expected to give at a meeting with the Lord Chancellor. It was a far from forgone conclusion, and she wrestled with her conscience. George loved Windsor and was as settled there as he could be given his parlous condition, and whenever the issue of a move came up, he seemed violently opposed to it. Yet what could the queen do now she had placed all her faith in the doctors? Pitt had every reason to hope that her handwringing was as protracted as possible; after all, if the Regent declared for the Whigs, he would be out of office.

The Privy Council now descended on Windsor to hear the medical evidence in favour of the journey. Charlotte was not present, preferring to retire to her own rooms and ruminate on what was becoming the most difficult decision she had ever made. All the time, she could only wonder at what Wales was discussing with the politicians and how it might play out should the Regency Bill be passed. Eventually, Charlotte made her decision: the royal household would relocate to Kew. When the Prince of Wales suggested that she should remain at Windsor, however, Charlotte ground her heels in hard. She might be kept from her husband by his doctors, but she wouldn't let the road lie between them too. Should Wales try to force her into staying at Windsor, she warned him to 'do it at your peril; where the King is, there shall I be'.

The king's doctors knew that he would not go to Kew quietly, even though physician Sir Lucas Pepys was of the opinion that the move might prove to be just what the sovereign needed. Instead, they decided that Charlotte and the princesses must be used to bait the hook, as George would definitely not leave Windsor if he believed they were still there. Charlotte was still fearful of the impact of the move to Kew on her husband, believing that the real motivation behind it was Wales's desire to be closer to the bright lights of London. As Frances Burney helped her anxious mistress to pack, Charlotte confided that 'the king's dislike was terrible to think of, and she could not foresee in what it might end.'[31] Burney was sure that Charlotte 'would have resisted the measure herself, but that she had determined to not to have upon her own mind any opposition to the opinion of the physicians.'[32] Charlotte's greatest fear was that her husband, when recovered, would not forgive her for moving him from Windsor.

Despite being 'drowned in tears',[33] Charlotte went along with the plan. The sobbing queen and her two eldest daughters, along with Lady Courtown, her lady-in-waiting, left the castle early the following morning. As the household saw them off, footmen, maids, and guards alike wept for the unknown future.

The plan worked. Unsurprisingly, George didn't accept his fate calmly, though the queen was told that he had. Instead, it took every ounce of persuasion that Pitt and the doctors possessed to convince him to follow his family to Kew, little knowing what fresh torments would soon be visited on him there.

A Fatal Precedent

At Kew, the White House was divided into two households by the Prince of Wales. He wrote the names of each inhabitant on the door of their intended rooms and the quarters given out were meagre, to say the least. The Queen shared her bedroom with Princess Augusta, whilst the king's medical team was given the use of the ground floor. The king himself was confined to a secure suite of rooms and his physicians controlled his access to other parts of the house. The rooms above George's were locked, to guarantee that he would not be disturbed by the sound of footsteps overhead. In addition to his doctors, he was tended by equerries Charles Hawkins and Colonel Goldsworthy, whilst the queen was surrounded by only her most trusted attendants. Chronicling it all was Frances Burney. Whilst the elder princesses remained with their mother, the younger princesses were placed in a house on Kew Green. They were cared for by their governesses and Lady Charlotte Finch, who was lodged in the Prince of Wales's house.

Upon his arrival at Kew, George headed for the queen's room, only to find her absent. He violently attacked his attendants and, from that day, his condition declined. When his doctors were called to make statements to the Privy Council, they remained confident that he would recover his wits, but they couldn't say when. It was obvious to everyone that they were simply hedging their bets. The monarch was in crisis.

Kew was the place at which the king and queen passed their darkest hours. With George's trusted royal physicians seemingly unable to help, Charlotte was at a loss. She had accepted the Lord Chancellor's request that she be responsible for the king, but in day-to-day terms it was his doctors who held sway. Charlotte's insular world had been entirely governed by her love of her husband and now he was sleepless, violent, and foamed at the mouth as he hurled abuse at her, accusing her of adultery and conspiracies against him. With nowhere else to turn, she listened with frantic interest to tales of Dr Francis Willis, a Lincolnshire clergyman turned physician. He had risen to prominence after curing the mania of the mother of Charlotte's Lady of the Bedchamber, Elizabeth Harcourt, who had come to Kew to sing his praises. Lady Harcourt was the daughter-in-law of the same Lord Harcourt who had arranged the king and queen's marriage all those years ago. She was one of Charlotte's most intimate friends and, with the king growing worse by the day, the queen

Freepost Plus RTKE-RGRJ-KTTX
Pen & Sword Books Ltd
47 Church Street
BARNSLEY
S70 2AS

DISCOVER MORE ABOUT PEN & SWORD BOOKS

Pen & Sword Books have over 4000 books currently available, our imprints include; Aviation, Naval, Military, Archaeology, Transport, Frontline, Seaforth and the Battleground series, and we cover all periods of history on land, sea and air.

Can we stay in touch? From time to time we'd like to send you our latest catalogues, promotions and special offers by post. If you would prefer not to receive these, please tick this box. ☐

We also think you'd enjoy some of the latest products and offers by post from our trusted partners: companies operating in the clothing, collectables, food & wine, gardening, gadgets & entertainment, health & beauty, household goods, and home interiors categories. If you would like to receive these by post, please tick this box. ☐

We respect your privacy. We use personal information you provide us with to send you information about our products, maintain records and for marketing purposes. For more information explaining how we use your information please see our privacy policy at www.pen-and-sword.co.uk/privacy. You can opt out of our mailing list at any time via our website or by calling 01226 734222.

Mr/Mrs/Ms ....

Address..

Postcode............................ Email address...

Website: www.pen-and-sword.co.uk Email: enquiries@pen-and-sword.co.uk
Telephone: 01226 734555 Fax: 01226 734438
Stay in touch: facebook.com/penandswordbooks or follow us on Twitter @penswordbooks

1. Her Most Gracious Majesty, Queen Charlotte. By Thomas Ryder, after Sir William Beechey. (Courtesy of the New York Public Library. Public domain)

2. Queen Charlotte and George, Prince of Wales. By Robert Pile, after Richard Houston. 1765. (Courtesy of the Wellcome Library, London, under Creative Commons Attribution only licence CC BY 4.0 http://creativecommons.org/licenses/by/4.0)

3. Queen Charlotte. By Richard Houston, after Johann Zoffany. (Courtesy of the Rijksmuseum, under Creative Commons Public Domain Dedication CC0 1.0 Universal licence. http://creativecommons.org/publicdomain/zero/1.0/deed.en)

4. George the III, King of Great Britain. By Anonymous. (Courtesy of the New York Public Library. Public domain)

Their most Sacred Majesties George the IIIrd and Queen Charlotte

with their Royal Highness George Prince of Wales, Frederick Bishop of Osnaburg, Prince William Henry, Princess Charlotte, Augusta Matilda, Prince Edward and Princess Sophia Augusta.

Above: 5. King George III and family. By Richard Earlom, after Johann Zoffany, 1871. (Courtesy of the Rijksmuseum, under Creative Commons Public Domain Dedication CC0 1.0 Universal licence. http://creativecommons.org/publicdomain/zero/1.0/deed.en)

Right: 6. Charlotte, Queen of Great Britain. By Anonymous. (Courtesy of the New York Public Library. Public domain)

Charlotte, Queen of Great Britain &c &c

7. The royal family of England in the year 1787. By Thomas Stothard, 1800. (From the British Cartoon Prints Collection (Library of Congress). No known restrictions on publication)

8. Charlotte, Queen of Great Britain, and the Princess Royal. By Valentine Green, after Benjamin West. (Courtesy of the Rijksmuseum, under Creative Commons Public Domain Dedication CC0 1.0 Universal licence. http://creativecommons.org/publicdomain/zero/1.0/deed.en)

Right: 9. Her Majesty Queen Charlotte. By Sir William Beechey, 1809. (Courtesy of the New York Public Library. Public domain)

Below: 10. *Royal Beneficence*. By Charles Howard Hodges, after Thomas Stothard, 1793. (Courtesy of the Rijksmuseum, under Creative Commons Public Domain Dedication CC0 1.0 Universal licence. http:// creativecommons.org/ publicdomain/zero/1.0/ deed.en)

HER MAJESTY QUEEN CHARLOTTE.

11. Queen Charlotte holding the baby Princess Charlotte, after Francis Cotes. (Courtesy of the Wellcome Library, London, under Creative Commons Attribution only licence CC BY 4.0 http://creativecommons.org/licenses/by/4.0)

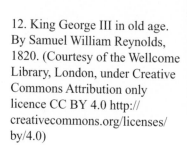

12. King George III in old age. By Samuel William Reynolds, 1820. (Courtesy of the Wellcome Library, London, under Creative Commons Attribution only licence CC BY 4.0 http://creativecommons.org/licenses/by/4.0)

Right: 13. Charlotte of Mecklenburg-Strelitz. By Henrik Roosing, 1789. (Courtesy of the Rijksmuseum, under Creative Commons Public Domain Dedication CC0 1.0 Universal licence. http://creativecommons.org/publicdomain/zero/1.0/deed.en)

Below: 14. *Taking Physick:- or- The News of Shooting the King of Sweden*. By James Gillray, 1792. The king and queen share a latrine as Pitt delivers bad news. (Courtesy of the Wellcome Library, London, under Creative Commons Attribution only licence CC BY 4.0 http://creativecommons.org/licenses/by/4.0)

CHARLOTTE,
Koningin van Engeland.

Above: 15. George III resuming royal power. By Benjamin West. (Courtesy of the National Gallery of Art. Public domain)

Left: 16. *The Apotheosis of Princes Octavius and Alfred*. By Sir Robert Strange, after Benjamin West, 1787. (Courtesy of the Wellcome Library, London, under Creative Commons Attribution only licence CC BY 4.0 http://creativecommons.org/licenses/by/4.0)

took her recommendation very seriously indeed. It seemed that Willis was her only option.

George's illness had a profound impact on Queen Charlotte. She began to suffer from severe insomnia and fits of nervous exhaustion, but she hoped against hope that Willis would work a miracle. Dr Willis arrived at Kew in the first week of December and immediately insisted on complete control over the life of George III. 'His MAJESTY is now chiefly under the care of Dr. WILLIS,' wrote *The Times* in December 1788. 'Those who know the *proximate* cause, as Physicians term it, of his Majesty's disorder, do not hesitate to say, that there is every reason to expect a recovery as soon as that cause can be removed.'[34] Willis was firmly of the opinion that the *proximate cause* was the stress of the king's workload, and that he alone could cure it.

Though Willis's unshakeable confidence in his own abilities soon caused tension within the monarch's medical team, that tension didn't seem initially to be reflected in the patient's condition. Almost immediately, Willis assured Queen Charlotte that his methods were working wonders on her husband, though Sir George Baker remained rightly circumspect. Charlotte's initial hopes for a miracle were dashed as George's torment continued and the White House, once his sanctuary, became his prison. Here he was straightjacketed and gagged or strapped into the infamous Coronation Chair, a restraining device into which Willis placed his regal patient whenever he got out of hand. Willis's treatment regime appears brutal to modern eyes but at the time his ice baths, leeches, blisters, and forced purges were actually seen as progressive. Not even Willis's most extreme treatments seemed to do any good and, as autumn wore on, a manic George told Charlotte that he loved her attendant Lady Pembroke, and that even Charlotte's dogs were more affectionate and adored than she had ever been.

The sexualised elements of the king's behaviour particularly upset Charlotte and were part of the reason for his being kept from her and their daughters without a chaperone. Courtier George Villiers found him 'indecent and obscene beyond description' towards maids and attendants, and he sent Lady Pembroke endless love letters. On one occasion, he burst naked into Charlotte's bedroom and threw her upon the bed, demanding that her attendants witness his sexual prowess. Though he was restrained immediately, it is little wonder that she insisted on locking her door when she slept.

George's ravings left Charlotte shattered and she grieved for him as though he was dead. Frances Burney watched in horror as the queen's hair turned grey and she lost more and more weight with each day that passed. For the sake of her children, Charlotte had to pretend that all was well, but she was struggling. Though she had the help of governesses and tutors with the younger children, Wales and York were a source of constant concern as the Regency power plays went on.

As December progressed, Willis began to allow the king limited supervised visits from the queen and Amelia, the couple's youngest daughter. At these meetings, physician Dr Thomas Gisborne wrote that George 'kiss'd [the queen's] hand passionately & said he held what was dearest to him in the world – the Queen kiss'd his hand, but could not speak.' When he took Amelia in a tight embrace, the infant princess squealed in terror. After these visits, George became more distressed than ever, and Charlotte followed suit. In a letter to Prince Augustus, Wales and York told their brother, 'His complaint, which is a total loss of all rationality … is now grown to such a pitch that he is a compleat [sic] lunatick [sic].'[35]

A second visit to the king resulted in him telling Charlotte that 'she was mad & had been so these three years, that He would on no Account admit Her to his Bed … for reasons he then improperly explained.' With George rambling about Lady

Pembroke, whom he called 'the Queen of Hearts', and telling Charlotte that their children were terrified of her, she retreated still further into melancholy solitude. When he began to ask to see her dog, Badine, rather than her, it was like a physical blow.

The circle around Charlotte grew ever smaller as her mood darkened and she saw precious few friends. Lady Elizabeth Harcourt was her rock, but Queen Charlotte was struggling. She had become a political pawn, accused of meddling with medical reports to help her Tory favourites at the expense of her husband's recovery, but such allegations were far from true. Charlotte did fear what the future might hold if Pitt was ousted by Wales's Whig friends, but she also held out hopes that her husband might yet recover. If he did, only to find his government chased out of office and power in the hands of the opposition, she feared that it might cause him to relapse.

Time was of the essence, and Charlotte had put all her trust in Dr Willis. Whether it was prayers, medicine, or simply the natural ebb and flow of his illness, as 1788 drew to a close, George began to rally. He was allowed to see his daughters and wife again and met them without his usual ravings and fury. He walked in the grounds, meek and polite, and Sir Lucas Pepys and the formidable Dr Willis brought hopes of a full return to health. Willis was assisted by his sons, also doctors, and together they were a team to be reckoned with. Multiple medical bulletins were sent to Parliament to advise on the king's condition, but even these became a weapon. When they noted even the slightest improvement in the condition of the king, Wales's Whig friends ventured to suggest that the queen had requested alterations to paint a more promising picture of her husband's recovery. They even suggested that Lady Harcourt should be cross-examined to ascertain just how sick the king really was and how much power Charlotte wielded. In fact, whilst Charlotte did request occasional amendments if she thought that the bulletins might compromise her husband's dignity, she never requested that they be turned into works of fiction.

All of this served to further deepen the queen's mistrust of her two eldest sons. Whilst she tried to protect George's privacy, Wales and York spread news of his perilous condition across the capital. Horace Walpole noted that the gossips of London were alight with news of 'fresh and grievous insults to the Prince [of Wales], who with the Duke of York are violently hindered by the Queen from even seeing their father.'[36] When supporters of the opposition added their voices to those calling for action to be taken, the king's friends rallied in defence of the royal family. 'I hear they want to disparage the queen,' thundered Lord Mansfield. 'Are they all insane? Why, her Majesty has more character than all of them together!'

When Dr Willis gave evidence to the Privy Council, he was as robust, forthright, and no-nonsense as ever. His methods were paying dividends, he argued, and would continue to do so. Conversely, Dr Warren was deliberately less forthcoming, suggesting that he was trying to preserve the king's dignity by holding back information. Pitt would have none of it and insisted that Warren share the undignified details he was keeping private. It was only then that Warren was forced to concede that no such details existed. In light of this, Willis won the victory – he was unquestionably the man who reigned over the king's treatment.

The Regency Bill was to be discussed in Parliament in mid-December, just as the queen received the most promising report yet concerning the health of her husband. It seemed as though the discussions in the House and George's recovery were racing one another, but Pitt believed that time had run out. Short of a miracle, the Regency would come to pass and the Prince of Wales would reign. Pitt would be removed from office, and the administration would be a Whig one.

Each time the king rallied, so too did Charlotte. Each time his condition worsened, she declined too, bearing the stress of her husband's illness more than anyone. Yet this time, Charlotte got her miracle once again and, as 1789 dawned, George was more like his old self than he had been in months. By the time Wales wrote to his mother urging her not to accept Parliament's offer of authority over the monarch's household should a Regency came to pass, the crisis was in its final days. The prince reminded her that the king always kept her out of politics, and warned darkly that Charlotte had come under the malign influence of puppet masters who hoped to manipulate the situation to their own ends:

> Before Your Majesty gives an answer to the application for your permission to place under your authority, the direction & appointment of the King's Household, thereby to disjoin from the difficult & arduous office which I am call'd upon to fill, the accustom'd & necessary support & dignity w[hic]h have hitherto belong'd to it. ... I have the same firm persuasion that those who under colour of respect & attachment to his royal Person have contriv'd this project for weakening and degrading the executive authority of the Empire will be considered by Him, as having risk'd the Peace & Happiness of his People for the purpose of their own interested ambition & as hav[in]g shaken the security of the Throne by establishing a fatal Precedent, which may hereafter be urged against his own authority, or be revived in various Pretences against the Rights of his Successors. ... How far those who are manifestly pressing both these objects, may be encourag'd in their purpose by Your Majesty's acceptance of the Powers of State denied to me, I will not presume to say. The Proposition itself has assumed the form of a

Resolution of Parliament, & therefore I leave unsaid much of what I feel & apprehend upon the subject. Your Majesty however will, I doubt not, do Me & Yourself the justice to weigh the opinions I form'd & entertain'd before the two Houses had adopted the present Plan & with those before you, which I have the honor to submit, will enable Your Majesty's own judgment to decide upon. Actuated as I am sure you will be, by your duty to my Father, & by your constant affection to Your Children I feel the firmest reliance on the Principle that nothing will ever prevail upon you to lend your countenance to any Councils, that can in the smallest degree be liable to even the suspicion or rumour of having consented to adopt measures, that were likely to interrupt in the slightest degree that harmony & affection that has ever invariably prevail'd.[37]

But the letter, which would not have changed Charlotte's mind anyway, came too late. She showed it to Pitt, who drafted a response that dismissed the prince's concerns. Queen Charlotte's reply was studied and guarded, whilst giving her son no quarter to argue that she had been unreasonable. Wales promised loyalty and affection and now she wanted him to prove it. The Regency had slipped through his fingers.

My dearest Son. Your Letter was delivered but a few minutes, before the Committee of both Houses came to me by my own appointment. Considering the Proposition as a Resolution of Parliament, I thought only one answer could be given to it: And, if Your suggestions had come in time, they are not sufficiently particular to furnish an alternative.

I saw Nothing in the address of the two Houses, but their Desire to charge me with a Trust, which, in all private Respects was my Duty before, with such Powers as seemed to them necessary for that purpose. That tender, and anxious Office I have endeavoured to perform, ever since the Melancholy occasion arose; and I have no views beyond it.

How the Kings Government is to be Administered, what provisions are to be made for replacing it in His hands, and what stile of dignity should attend His Person in the mean Time are considerations, upon which I can form no adequate Judgement.

If the care of so great a Person is thought by the Public necessarily to draw after it an establishment, which is really capable of being abused in the manner You represent, I must Consider Even that circumstance as a mark of Their confidence, that no such abuse will be attempted.

Conscious of my Claim to Your Affection and Confidence, I believe You without hesitation, when You assure me, that You depend upon my Duty to the King, and my constant affection to my Children, for preserving harmony & mutual kindness in the Family. Nor can I omit to thank You from my Heart for this solemn promise, that I shall continue the constant Object of Your wish to cherish and promote it.

When it shall please God to restore the King to Us and the Nation, I will not fail to lay before Him Every Paper, and make every other representation, which You may wish to convey through me: for I shall resume with joy in the Office, in which I have always delighted, of Conciliating and maintaining the harmony of my Family.

> How long our Common calamity may last,
> God, who inflicts it, alone can foresee. In the mean
> time You will Easily conceive, how much of my
> Consolation must depend on preserving the Affection
> of my Family.[38]

The Regency Bill was under debate in January and February 1789, but with every day that passed, the king was recovering. He sat with the queen and Badine without incident and even attended a private family gathering in honour of the queen's birthday in February. When a terrified Frances Burney fled from him in the grounds at Kew, the king caught up with her only to assure her that he was well once more, and that she must never fear him again. She was soon to witness a scene that appeared to prove it.

> I had this morning the highest gratification, the purest
> feeling of delight, I have been regaled with for many
> months: I saw, from the road, the King and Queen,
> accompanied by Dr. Willis, walking in Richmond
> Gardens, near the farm, arm in arm! – It was a
> pleasure that quite melted me, after a separation so
> bitter, scenes so distressful – to witness such harmony
> and security![39]

By the time Burney made her report, there was no question that George would soon be well enough to resume his duties. When the medical bulletin announced the 'entire cessation of his Majesty's illness'[40] on 26 February 1789, the ensuring celebrations ensured that Willis's transformation from doctor to celebrity was complete. Two months later, he featured in three portraits at the Royal Academy exhibition.

Charlotte had lost so much weight that her stays now hung off her, but with the news that George was recovering, she resolved to make herself well again. The family returned to Windsor on 14 March amid a tidal wave of public love, the like of which they hadn't seen since their earliest days together. They had survived the storm.

A Smart Little Tussle

The Regency Bill was yanked off the Parliamentary slate and across the country, public festivities were held to celebrate George's recovery. The king spent his convalescence devouring reports of his illness and studying the behaviour of those close to him during his confinement. His preoccupation with who had been loyal – Pitt, for one – and who had not began to prey on Charlotte. His temper seemed frayed, and the queen was convinced that even the slightest upset might cause a relapse, so she became more timid than ever around her husband. She did not exhibit the same timidity with her sons, and it was with thin-lipped disapproval that she agreed to allow Wales and York to enjoy a short audience with their father towards the end of February. Though the meeting was held in Charlotte's private apartments, she took her leave with scarcely a word to the young men.

Surprisingly, given what he had been through, George III soon began to entertain thoughts of a trip to Hanover, where he would seek husbands for his daughters. Of course, the idea of such a visit was fanciful at best and George was certainly neither mentally nor physically capable of undertaking what would be an arduous trip, but the more he thought about it, the more determined he became. Upon hearing this, the Prince of Wales pressed harder to see his father and even asked Charlotte to give the king a letter in which he and York set down their concerns, but the queen refused to do any such thing. Instead, she handed them a letter in which the king explained that he was too ill to receive them. Believing that Charlotte was responsible for this, the fallout was calamitous.

Charlotte and the Prince of Wales had a stand-up row. He accused her of conspiring to blacken his name and Charlotte, who had seemed so meek and unassuming when she had first come onto the radar of the British royal family, went through the roof. Driven to distraction by her worries for the king, she gave full rein to her temper and refused to let the prince speak. Instead, she ordered him out of the house, telling him in no uncertain terms that she wouldn't convey messages from either himself or York to the king. When the Duke of York narrowly escaped injury in a duel with Colonel Charles Lennox, the queen was unmoved. She simply said that York must be to blame for the argument that led to the duel, for she couldn't imagine he was innocent.

> The Prince of Wales has had a smart little tussle with the Queen, in which they came to strong and open declarations of hostility. He told her that she had connected herself with his enemies, and had entered into plans for destroying and disgracing him and all her children, and that she countenanced misrepresentations of his conduct to the King, and prevented the explanations he wished to give. She was violent and lost her temper; and the conversation ended, I believe, by her saying that she would not be the channel of anything that either he or the Duke of York had to say to the King, and that the King did not mind what either he or the Duke of York either did or said or thought. I do not think such a conversation well judged on the part of the Prince.[41]

To drive the point home, when the queen planned a concert to celebrate her husband's recovery, neither of her eldest sons were invited. She tried to cushion the blow – or to give the impression that she was trying to – by telling them that they could attend if they wanted to, whilst pointing out that the concert was intended as a thank you to loyal Tories who had stood by George throughout his illness. Given his sons' opposition sympathies, she could see no reason whatsoever why they would wish to be present.

The Prince of Wales had a temper as hot as that of his mother, and his brothers and friends constantly warned him that he should show more circumspection. The king complained of Wales's 'want of even common civility towards the Queen',[42] yet he showed no sign of changing. He had already caused no end of trouble with his constant begging to pay off his debts and the rumours of his secret marriage to the Catholic Maria Fitzherbert, and any further communication between him and his mother would have been incendiary.

Instead, it was left to the Duke of York, the king's favourite son, to try to pour oil on the troubled waters. It was he who attempted to convince Charlotte that this wasn't a time for partisan loyalties, but for a nationwide celebration where everyone could rejoice as one. Charlotte wasn't having it for a moment. She told her son plainly that the concert was for friends of the monarch, and Wales and York were anything but. As if that wasn't insult enough, the pious and family-focused Charlotte might have excluded her eldest sons – one of whom was heir to the throne – but she *did* invite Princess Sophia, the daughter of Prince William Henry and Maria Walpole, the Duke and Duchess of Gloucester. The Duke was George's brother and when he married the commoner Maria, George banished them both from his sight. To have their child present whilst her own sons were not invited was a studied insult on the part of the queen. This time, even York lost his cool. Even if Charlotte went down on her knees and begged him – which she would never do – he would not attend.

The episode of the concert was a clear indication of the impact of the king's illness on Charlotte. She was not a firebrand, concealing a hot temper under a façade of placid calm for years, but had been changed by George's illness just as surely as he had. One of the reasons Charlotte had been considered the perfect bride was her lack of political ambition and, from the very day of their first meeting, she and George had clearly delineated roles. George was the statesman, Charlotte the faithful keeper of the flame, and never the twain would meet. Now, years later and faced with the very real prospect of one day serving as Regent, the queen had no idea of how to do it, no wish to do it, and an ambitious son snapping at her heels. Combined with the stress of simply living with George's condition day in, day out, the pressure was immense.

George's recovery did much to mend the queen's spirits. Early in March, she and the king slept in the same bed for the first time in months and at a grand Drawing Room in the Queen's House, Charlotte was a picture of regal composure. Seated in a chair of state beside her husband, she literally glittered, her gown covered in clusters of pearls and diamonds. As the assembly passed by her to be received, she warmly welcomed those who had stayed loyal in the king's hour of crisis. For those who had thrown their weight behind Wales, the reception was considerably more muted. Yet Charlotte was in a celebratory mood when she and her daughters travelled through London by night to witness the illuminations that lit the darkness on 10 March, the day that Parliament sent her an official congratulatory message on the occasion of George's recovery. All of the city had come out to celebrate George III, it seemed, and only Carlton House, the home of the Prince of Wales, appeared a little subdued. Charlotte became almost giddy, on one occasion lightly slapping the bottom of the Honourable Georgina Townshend and telling the startled young lady, 'I believe you was never whipped by a queen before!' She issued celebratory medals to her ladies, on which was inscribed *Vive le Roi*, and tried to convince herself that the crisis had passed.

Despite her high spirits, Charlotte still feared that George might suffer a relapse, or that his physical weakness might yet be the undoing of him. When he insisted on attending a three-hour service of thanksgiving on 23 April, both the queen and the royal doctors tried to convince him that he should stay at home. George wouldn't hear of it and his appearance thrilled the waiting public. Though Pitt was cheered all the way to St Paul's, Fox and the Prince of Wales were booed as they passed. Wales and York compounded the disapproval by laughing together at the service as 5,000 children sang the 100th psalm, leading one eyewitness to comment, 'I believe the King's mind is torn to pieces by his sons.' In Charlotte's opinion, though, there was one indisputable fact: if Wales's betrayal had not come as a surprise given his closeness to the Regency, the perceived betrayal of the Duke of York was the one that really cut deep. York and his father had been close from boyhood and York was certainly the king's favourite. In supporting his elder brother's claim to the Regency, he had incurred Charlotte's wrath above anyone.

The turmoil Charlotte experienced during her husband's illness had left its mark in other ways too. When she sat for the young Thomas Lawrence, the painter found it difficult to capture the contemplative, solemn appearance of his subject. It was all he could do to persuade the queen to cooperate at all, and she agreed to just a single sitting. When the painting was finished, Charlotte's decision not to purchase it came as a great blow to Lawrence's hopes, as well as those of the princesses, who were great fans of his. The portrait was destined to become acclaimed as one of Lawrence's finest works, but it remained in his personal collection until his death.

Still brooding over York's behaviour, the king and queen and their three eldest daughters took an extended trip to Weymouth, where 'the Queen walks about with only a Lady and goes into the shops,' according to Mrs Harcourt. Here the king could convalesce and the queen could breathe again, whilst together they hosted a ball to celebrate their wedding anniversary. It put some much-needed space between Charlotte and her eldest sons and eventually, cheered by their shared love of the king, time soothed the hurt on all sides. But it was far from the last time Charlotte and her children would clash.

That Tyger Nation

For the next few years, the royal family and government tentatively allowed themselves to believe that the danger had passed. In France, on the other hand, Charlotte's correspondent Marie Antoinette knew nothing but danger. Though the two queens had never met, Charlotte had long worried 'that the poor unhappy Queen will fall a victim to that tyger nation'.[43] She was right.

More than a decade separated the births of the British and French queens, but in many other ways there were close similarities. Both had been brides in an arranged marriage, neither was considered a beauty, and both were utterly innocent of the world into which they were plunged. Charlotte struggled to connect with her mother-in-law, whilst Marie Antoinette was at the mercy of gossiping courtiers and favourites, and on a more prosaic level, both had an enduring love of jewellery and a shared affection for the bucolic life. Queen Charlotte devoted herself to tending the grounds at Frogmore, greatly expanded after the initial purchase of the Crown lease on Frogmore Farm, renamed Amelia Lodge by Charlotte. In 1792, she added the lease on Great Frogmore to her portfolio, and had the grounds joined. She referred to Frogmore as Little Paradise, and tending its estate – along with that of Kew – was always her preferred therapy. 'I go slow,' she admitted to Prince Augustus, 'In order to make the pleasure last the longer.'[44] She threw herself into the care of her gardens and menagerie with all the gusto of Marie Antoinette playing shepherdess at the Petit Trianon.

Yet whilst England was politically relatively stable, save the odd bit of radical sabre-rattling that got louder during the reign of the Prince Regent, France had taken a very different turn. Across the sea, the Bourbon royal family had been deposed and dethroned and though Charlotte had sent clothes and essentials to her friend, she could offer no other help. The opportunity to save the family had been missed.

'Ancient history can hardly produce anything more barbarous and cruel than our neighbours in France,'[45] wrote Charlotte, and when Marie Antoinette was put to death, plans for a celebration to mark the anniversary of George III's Coronation were cancelled out of respect. Yet Charlotte was no doubt glad that in her own home, things remained settled. Unfortunately, that didn't last.

One Damned German Frau

For all his courtesans, actresses, and even that illegal wife, the Prince of Wales always knew that one day he would have to make an official marriage. The line of succession rested on his shoulders and Charlotte lobbied hard for her niece, Louise of Mecklenburg-Strelitz, to marry him, but he was understandably reluctant to wed his mother's favourite. Wales's scheming mistress, Lady Jersey, reminded him that a marriage would settle his debts, so eventually it was agreed that he would marry Caroline of Brunswick, his paternal cousin. After all, as Wales sighed, 'One damned German frau is as good as another.' But Charlotte disagreed. Just as she never liked Caroline's mother, Princess Augusta, nor did she like Caroline either. In fact, when Charlotte's widowed brother had considered marrying Caroline himself, Charlotte was quick to take up her pen. She had heard all sorts of gossip about the princess's behaviour and morals, and she had plenty to say about it.

'[Caroline's] passions are so strong that the Duke himself said that she was not to be allowed even to go from one room to another without her Governess, and that when she dances, this lady is obliged to follow her for the whole of the dance to prevent her from making an exhibition of herself,' Charlotte warned, giving credence to every bit of groundless gossip she had heard about the spirited princess. 'There, dear brother is a woman I do not recommend at all.'[46]

The marriage was a disaster from the off. The prince complained that his bride smelled, and she retorted that he was nothing like the handsome man in his portraits. Wales excused himself from their first meetings and fled for his mother's rooms, where he drowned his sorrows in a glass of brandy. The only good thing that came of it as far as Charlotte was concerned was the birth of her first grandchild, Princess Charlotte Augusta of Wales, who was named in honour of both her grandmothers. Within months of her birth in 1796, the Prince and Princess of Wales had split up for good.

The strain of trying to keep the Wales household together was particularly damaging to the king. It was he who received impassioned letters from both husband and wife and though Charlotte never liked her daughter-in-law, George certainly did. He did all he could to keep the couple together, but it was a hopeless mission. Even worse, every twist and turn in the failing royal marriage was played out in public, as arguments between the prince and princess, and the princess and Lady Jersey, the mistress who had been installed as Caroline's attendant, found their way into the press. Lady Jersey was a close friend of the queen, so it was no surprise whose side Charlotte came down on. Whilst George was determined to supervise the education of his granddaughter and ensure that she didn't end up a weapon in her parents' war, Charlotte distanced herself from the split. She certainly loved her little namesake though, and gave her some of her own old childhood toys, including a gold mouse with bejewelled eyes. She also kept a grandmotherly eye on the infant's health, warning Wales that the child was 'plagued with her teeth & I fancy that a very exact attention to the dyet [sic] prescribed for her will prevent all uneasiness.'[47]

The queen had never wanted the marriage between Wales and Caroline in the first place, but she was sorry that it had ended so unhappily. She had not, however, done anything to help, but had instead followed the example of her own mother-in-law. Despite receiving the Princess of Wales with cool detachment and encouraging her daughters to follow suit, when Charlotte learned that Caroline had nicknamed her 'Old Snuffy', she took the insult to heart. Whilst the king encouraged his son to salvage the marriage, the queen was rather less imploring. It should come as no surprise that Wales hoped his mother might be able to convince the king that Caroline was the enemy, but George was too focused on keeping his granddaughter out of it. If that meant he was to be torn in two, it was a risk he was willing to take.

The Prince of Wales whined constantly to Charlotte about his wife, and she internalised every complaint, shouldering the fresh burden alongside her own anxiety. She wanted nothing more than to see father and son reconciled, but the more ground the king gave to Caroline of Brunswick, the less likely it became. These domestic dramas combined with worry about the state of a nation at war in which food prices were so high that the poor were starving. Mobs protested in the streets, their shouts audible in the Queen's House, and the king and queen were heckled when they went out in public. All of this helped to drive Charlotte back into the melancholy to which she was so often subject.

Yet whilst Wales was trying to escape his spouse, the royal daughters were pushing in the other direction. Had George III not fallen ill, it's likely that they would have been fully exposed to the royal marriage mart. Instead, they inhabited an insular world in which their mother reigned supreme. They were usually impeccably well-behaved and mindful of Charlotte's ever-worsening temper, yet the queen had a far more useful weapon than the lash of her tongue – her silence. The princess' subgoverness, Mary Hamilton, warned her charges that they should hope never to incur the queen's indifference, as 'scarcely a greater misfortune can befall [them].'[48]

As the years passed, this insular world would become infamous, nicknamed 'the Windsor nunnery' by one of the princesses themselves, and it began early. The Princess Royal, Charlotte's eldest daughter, became her secretary and was rumoured by her sisters to be their mother's spy. 'I heard many a story that the Princess Royal has repeated to the Queen,'[49] Princess Sophia confided to the Prince of Wales, with a wry pen. Ironically, Royal never wanted the role in the first place. Instead, she felt forced to toe the line by Charlotte's fearsome temper, 'which hourly grows worse, to which [Royal] is not only obliged to submit, but to be absolutely a slave.'[50] Though this might suggest that the queen ruled her daughters with a rod of iron rather than motherly love, she certainly loved her children, even when they were behaving badly. The princesses remained at home whilst the princes, with the exception of Wales, could pursue careers and travel, so they were by necessity closer to their mothers than their brothers could ever be. Charlotte took great pride in their talents, which ranged from art to music to botany, in the case of the Princess Royal. This was something that the two women could share and, as Royal grew into a woman, she proved to have a real aptitude for the science.

It was hardly surprising that Royal, by now a grown woman, wanted out. She had received her first marital interest as far back as 1782, but George was determined that his daughter would finish her education before she married anyone. With the king's illness, the chance of another suitor calling became ever more remote, and it seemed as though Royal would be stuck at home forever.

Things were made considerably worse when Ferdinand Augustus of Württemberg showed an interest in Princess Augusta, Royal's younger sister. There was no question of the younger sister marrying before the elder and, with nobody asking after Royal, it began to look as though the princesses would never leave their parents' side.

In 1795, nobody was more surprised than Royal to hear that Crown Prince Frederick of Württemberg was making enquiries about her availability. His marriage to George III's late niece, Augusta of Brunswick-Wolfenbüttel, had ended in allegations of spousal abuse and homosexual trysts, so he was by far the last person the king and queen might choose for their daughter. Yet Royal was determined, if not to marry Frederick, then to marry *anyone*. She begged her parents to reconsider and, in 1797, got her wish. Queen Charlotte lost her secretary and Württemberg gained its future queen. Royal's place as her mother's confidante was taken by Augusta, her younger sister. Lively, optimistic, and full of vivacity, she was the polar opposite to the introspective Princess Royal.

Charlotte made her daughter's wedding gown with her own hand, even capitulating to Royal's preferred colour scheme of white and silver, which went against her own choice of white and gold. At the ceremony, Charlotte wept happy tears to see her eldest daughter become a bride and when she finally left for the continent, both the king and queen were observed to be broken-hearted to say goodbye. They closed the summer with a return to Weymouth, where the Prince of Wales 'found the dear Queen quite well & looking better than she has done in my opinion for months & years.'[51]

Perhaps most surprising of all, when the Prince of Wales grew despondent at the collapse of his relationship with his secret wife, Maria Fitzherbert, it was Queen Charlotte who pressed them to reunite. She didn't acknowledge that any marriage had taken place, but she knew as well as anyone that Maria was a stabilising influence on Wales. She sent a note to Maria asking her to reconsider the relationship and Maria capitulated. It wouldn't last, but as the century drew to a close, things were finally looking up.

A Most Severe Trial

The nineteenth century started with a very literal bang, when James Hatfield took a shot at George III as he entered his box at Drury Lane Theatre on 15 May 1800. The queen was a few paces behind her husband and, though the shot missed its target, she was understandably shaken. It was a terrible start to a new century and in 1801, things got even worse when the king came down with a fever so severe that Willis and his sons, John, Thomas, and Robert, were called. Within days, the king's condition had deteriorated to such an extent that Charlotte and Wales were summoned to his bedside, and Willis admitted that he feared for his patient's life. When George regained consciousness, he seemed determined to hoodwink the Willises into believing that he had no need of their care, but they were too experienced for that. They met his determination to perform his official duties with blistering and bleeding, but this time George wasn't going to capitulate so easily. He dismissed the doctors, then made for Kew.

The king's escape gave Willis all the proof he needed that the monarch's madness had returned. Overwork and worry about matters of state had occasioned a relapse, he told Charlotte and the prime minister, Henry Addington, and they gave him permission to follow the sovereign and detain him by force if necessary.

Once again, George III was confined to the White House at Kew, denied the right to see his family, and subjected to traumatic treatments. On this occasion though, he was not so deranged that he couldn't threaten a shutdown. George declared to Lord Eldon that unless he was permitted to 'go over to the house where the Queen and his family were, no earthly consideration should induce him to sign his name to any paper or to do one act of government whatever.'

The Willises had no choice but to relent and, with regular scheduled audiences with his wife and daughters, the king began to recover. In the early summer, George was able to enjoy a restorative trip to Weymouth, a place his wife only tolerated, but his relapse had left Charlotte constantly looking out for any sign of distress. The king, meanwhile, could no longer bear to even look at the White House, where he had spent so many happy days when he and his wife were newlyweds. Here he had indulged his love of agriculture and Charlotte her love of botany, but now every memory was one of horror. He had the White House torn down. Today, a sundial marks the spot where it once stood.

The last years of the eighteenth century had been extraordinarily stressful for George III and the nineteenth promised no let-up. The failed marriage of the Prince and Princess of Wales had long been a source of unhappiness for the king. With their separation, the fate of their only child, Charlotte, had become a weapon in both their hands, and George seemed to be constantly butting heads with his son over the little girl's care. If family affairs were tense, in the rest of the world things were little better, but as war raged on the continent, Charlotte did all she could to provide a settled home.

Life at Windsor, which carried none of the traumatic memories associated with Kew and the doctors Willis, should have been close to idyllic, but George's health worries were never far from Charlotte's mind. After his decision to have the White House torn down, George sought a promise that none of the Willis family would ever be allowed to treat him again. Regardless of how many illustrious patients they gained as a result of their much-trumpeted success in the case of the British king,[52] the very thought of seeing the Willises again was enough to terrify him.

In February 1804, Charlotte's worst fears were realised when George fell ill once more. Mindful of the promise she had made to her husband, Charlotte did not call the Willis family to his side, but summoned instead Sir Lucas Pepys and Sir Francis Milman, who was already treating her for a cold. Should any of the doctors Willis be forced upon the king again, warned the Duke of Kent, it would likely cause the king to take 'up a rooted prejudice against the Queen, for that no argument however strong, no proof however direct, would be sufficient, after his recovery, to persuade him that her Majesty had not been privy to the doctors Willis being placed about his person.'

Prime Minister Henry Addington had other ideas. He had taken over the premiership from Pitt in 1801 and had been spared the horrendous scenes at Kew. As far as he knew, Willis had healed the king, so with that in mind, he called in John and Robert Willis, only to have them turned away by the Dukes of Cumberland and Kent. They preferred to trust their own choice of Dr Samuel Foart Simmons, the renowned physician to St Luke's Hospital for Lunatics, and his son, Richard.

Dr Simmons's methods were no more humane than those of Willis, and once again the king was straightjacketed, blistered, and gagged. This time, Charlotte was determined not to bow under pressure, and a letter sent by Princess Mary to the Prince of Wales late one February evening in 1804 gives a glimpse into her state of mind:

> Such a *day* I never went through in my life. The poor Queen keeps up wonderfully but the *trial* is a most severe one. ... I am happy to add mama's health has not suffered yet from all *she* has gone through in mind & body since *we are* come to town.[53]

As the months passed, the king grew ever more resentful and angry towards his wife. Equerry Colonel McMahon wrote that

He manifests the greatest aversion to the Queen & is quite outrageous with her. He states publickly [sic] before his sons & the Princesses that his arrangement is this: he'll never have any connexion more with the Queen, that he'll fit up the Great Lodge in the Park entirely for himself, & take Lady Pembroke into keeping who shall live there with his two youngest daughters, but that if Lady Pembroke declines his offer [he] will then make it to the Dss. of Rutland.[54]

Charlotte could never quite forgive his husband for the words he uttered in his delirium.

By the time George was well enough to visit Weymouth, the relationship between the couple was more strained than ever. George still threatened to take a mistress and society was rife with gossip that he had become obsessed with sex, even making lewd advances to women in the street. Sir Robert Wilson reported that the king was visibly unwell whilst in Weymouth, his behaviour lurching between statesmanlike, good-humoured, and frenzied. He made loud and public pronouncements on the values or otherwise of politicians that left Charlotte and her daughters on edge, fearing what was to come next. In the evening, the queen had the princesses stay in her bedroom until she was certain that the king was safely in his quarters, a sure sign of her continued concern.

'I have never been able to ascertain the cause of the Queen's great disgust for the king,' wrote Wilson, 'But no doubt she must have very good reason to resist nature, her duty, the advice of physicians & the entreaties of Ministers.'[55] The trip to Weymouth ended with the king and queen quarrelling violently, their helpless daughters watching in tears. The situation was at crisis point.

As if this wasn't enough, the king's behaviour towards the princesses was changing too. George had always been a caring father to his daughters, particularly Amelia, whom he affectionately called Emily, but an incident in Southampton perfectly illustrates the permanent change that had come over his character. Amelia had been ill with tuberculosis of the knee for some time and had only recently become well enough to resume her beloved horse rides. Whilst riding with her father and politician George Rose, she suffered a nasty fall and was reluctant to remount. The king's reaction left her reeling.

> [We] were interrupted by the Princess Amelia (who, with the other Princesses, was riding behind us) getting a most unfortunate fall. The horse, on cantering down an inconsiderable hill, came on his head, and threw her Royal Highness flat on her face. She rose, without any appearance of being at all hurt, but evidently a good deal shaken; and notwithstanding an earnest wish to avoid occasioning the slightest alarm, was herself not desirous of getting on horseback again; but the King insisted that she should, if at all hurt, get into one of the carriages and return to Cuffnells to be bled, or otherwise mount another horse and ride on. She chose the latter, and rode to Southampton, where she lost some blood unknown to the King. I hazarded an advice, that no one else would do, for her Royal Highness's return, which was certainly not well received, and provoked a quickness from his Majesty that I experienced in no other instance. He observed that he could not bear that any of his family should want courage. To which I replied, I hoped his majesty would excuse me if I said I thought a proper attention to prevent the ill effects of an accident that had happened, was no symptom of a want of courage. He then said with some warmth:– 'Perhaps it may be so; but I thank God there is but one of my children who wants courage; – and I will not name HIM, because he is to succeed me.'[56]

Charlotte knew that her husband was relapsing, but she responded to even the slightest suggestion of illness with frantic denials. She was so aware of George's condition that even when he was in good health, she rarely allowed herself the pleasure of relaxing. Her mood and wellbeing were in constant flux, and her weight yo-yoed from painfully thin to heavily overweight, just as her spirits prevaricated between melancholy and placid. She was never as joyful as she had been in youth again, and always a little afraid of what might be round the next corner.

Lord Malmesbury noted that, as late as December 1804, 'The Queen will never receive the King without one of the princesses being present, – never says, in reply a word, – piques herself on this discreet silence – and, when in London, locks the door of her *white room* (her boudoir) against him.'[57] She welcomed Wales back to her side, needing all the support she could get as the husband she had once adored changed beyond all recognition. They no longer travelled in a carriage together without a chaperone, and she refused to spend time with the king unless other people were present. Her temper, always stretched, was frayed beyond repair.

Gone was the fun-loving king who had rolled on the carpets with his children, and gone too was the devoted husband and best friend who had been Charlotte's constant companion. Now she had only her daughters, and if suitors occasionally came seeking their hand, they were rebuffed. She made only one exception to this seemingly unshakeable rule. When her brother, Charles II, Grand Duke of Mecklenburg-Strelitz, enquired about a possible bride for his eldest son, George, the queen promised to consider it.

The Sun of Our Days Was Set

George III and Queen Charlotte were parents to fifteen children, two of whom did not survive to adulthood. The lives of their daughters were filled with rumours of illegitimate babies and secret weddings,[58] but compared to those of their brothers, they were what we might politely term insular. After George's first period of illness, the fiercely protective Charlotte did whatever she could to prevent him from even considering the issue of marriages for their daughters, believing that the strain would be too great. George himself was little better, tormented as he was by the memory of his sister, Caroline Matilda, and her unhappy fate in Denmark.

Caroline Matilda's miserable teenage marriage to Christian VII of Denmark had ended with the execution of the queen's lover and her imprisonment and early death. It's no surprise that when the first interest in George's daughters came from the Danish court, George dismissed it out of hand. This set the pattern for refusal after refusal, which left the sisters despairing.

The king periodically mused on the possibility of a trip to Europe to scope out possible matches for the girls, but these were never more than pipe dreams. Royal alone escaped the 'Windsor nunnery' before the portcullis came down, and she had been so desperate to do so that she had suffered from a bout of depression before permission was received. For the other girls, there would be no such escape.

In 1805, Charlotte's brother Charles wrote to his sister regarding a possible marriage between his son, George, and one of the British princesses. Charlotte sent the letter to her husband with a carefully worded covering note in which she assured him that

> I have never named the Subject to any of the Princesses, for I have made it [a] rule to avoid a Subject in which I know their oppinions [sic] differ with Your Majesty's, for every one of them have at different Times assured me that, happy as they are, they should like to settle if they could, and I feel I cannot blame them.[59]

With access to the princesses so fiercely guarded, this might seem like quite a turnaround, but Charlotte had less concerns about a marriage that would be a family affair. By marrying one of her daughters to her nephew, the benefits for Charlotte's familial duchy would be financially, socially, and politically immense. The chosen daughter would make her marital home in a place that was familiar to Charlotte and where there were few potential unknowns. George agreed to consider the possibility, but only if the would-be bride was entirely behind the project.

'My dearest Queen,' he wrote, 'After having had the good fortune to possess such a treasure come from Strelitz, it is impossible for me to hesitate a moment, if my daughters wish to marry, to declare I would like to see them allied with this house above all others in Germany.' Nevertheless, he admitted that 'I cannot deny that I have never wished to see any of them marry; I am happy in their company and do not in the least want a separation,' but he would not stand in the way should one of his daughters wish to marry the Hereditary Prince of Mecklenburg-Strelitz.

Charlotte was heartened by the thought of a wedding in the family. She suggested that the prince come to England after the royal family had returned from a planned trip to Weymouth. If the visit was undertaken as a private family one, it could be both cost-effective and relatively under the radar. What the queen had reckoned without was the opinion of the prospective groom. To her surprise, none of the princesses appealed to him and he declined the opportunity, dashing Charlotte's hopes that he might make a wife of Princess Amelia. Amelia, however, had other romantic irons in the fire.

Princess Amelia had first met Charles FitzRoy, her father's equerry, when he was charged with attending her during a bout of illness. When she fell sick in Weymouth, at the end of the holiday it was agreed that Amelia should stay at the coast for a while to benefit from the fresh air. FitzRoy was to attend her, along with Jane Gomm, a maid-of-honour. The dashing son of Baron Southampton, FitzRoy's closeness to the king had earned him the nickname 'Prince Charles'. Despite being twenty-one years older than Princess Amelia, they soon grew close. They hung back together on horse rides with the king and could always be found at the same card table in the evening. Amelia's sister, Princess Mary, soon noticed that something was going on.

When Amelia heard that Jane Gomm and Mary had been discussing her friendship with FitzRoy, she was furious. She became even more angry when Charlotte warned her about 'riding near the King, and not to keep behind', making it clear that she had heard all about the couple too. In fact, Miss Gomm had clued the queen in about the princess and the equerry in 1803, expecting her to take a firm hand. Instead, the queen swerved the issue of the clandestine romance altogether and simply advised her daughter that she must be more respectful of Miss Gomm and not lose her temper again. On one point, however, she was unequivocal: Amelia must not make any complaints to the king, who could not on any account be upset. She knew Amelia well, for the king had always been her champion. Little Emily had come along when he was mourning his sons and he clung to her through his trials. As her own health began to fail, the two of them would decline together.

Mistrustful of her sisters, Amelia took her complaints to the Prince of Wales. Though Wales and the queen could fight like cat and dog, Amelia knew that nobody else could soothe the queen when her temper got the better of her. In this case, however, there was nothing that he could do.

Things were no better for Princess Elizabeth, who spoke for all her unmarried sisters when she told the Prince of Wales sadly that 'we go on vegetating, as we have done for the last twenty years of our lives.' No wonder she still allowed herself to dream of a happy ending when the Duke of Kent's friend, Louis Philippe, the Duke of Orléans, made overtures towards her. The Duke's life as a schoolteacher in Twickenham was a far cry from what it might have been if not for the French Revolution, but Elizabeth didn't care. It didn't matter either way, because when news of his interest reached the queen, she stamped on it. Elizabeth wrote despairingly to Wales, letting him know what had happened:

> I was asked by the Queen whether I knew [of Louis Philippe's interest and] I had flattered myself that from my constant steady attendance upon my mother, with my natural openness of character, I had hoped she would have had confidence in me at my time of life, but finding alas to my grief that was not the case I thought it more honourable by her and just towards myself to let her know I was not ignorant of what had passed, with my sentiments and feelings upon it.
>
> If there is no possibility of the [proposal] now, I only entreat of you as the person, both from inclination, duty and affection we must look up to, that you will not dash the cup of happiness from my lips.[60]

Charlotte would never countenance a marriage to the Catholic Duke, and remained adamant that her husband would not allow it either. Elizabeth told Wales darkly that she had learned that a great many proposals 'had been brought forward and rejected without a word from us, and therefore we all felt the sun of our days was set.' Though she said no more, the implication was clear. Someone, most likely the queen, had dashed the princesses' marital hopes before the women even knew that they existed.

Although all of the princesses could invoke the Royal Marriages Act once they were over the age of 25 and pursue a wedding even without parental consent, none would. Queen Charlotte ruled her children with her hot temper and the constant threat that any upset could permanently cost the king his sanity. She knew full well that her daughters thought far too much of their father to put him at risk. When Elizabeth wrote that '[Charlotte] always said, that did she let herself once go she could never conduct herself as she ought', she wasn't exaggerating. Charlotte tamped her temper down because she had to, but when she let it out it was a sight to behold.

Whilst the princesses were being urged to do all they could to avoid upsetting their father, it seemed as though their brothers were going in the other direction. If it wasn't bad enough that Prince Augustus had married in defiance of the Royal Marriages Act and seen that marriage annulled, the Duke of Clarence was happily ensconced with actress Dora Jordan, and the gossip columns still seethed with all the latest scandal from the Prince of Wales. Twenty years after his clandestine and illegal marriage to Maria Fitzherbert, the couple had been on and off so many times that even the Vatican got involved. To further embarrass the family, he had spent years and a small fortune trying to end his marriage to Caroline of Brunswick too. Despite false rumours that she had delivered an illegitimate child, very true accusations of adultery on both sides, and lists of lovers for both the prince and princess that would fill reams of paper, the king would not countenance a divorce. Instead, the couple were yoked together in mutual loathing, with their daughter a pawn in their arguments.

Caroline's mother, Duchess Augusta, had never got along with her sister-in-law, Queen Charlotte, whom she regarded as 'an envious and intriguing spirit'.[61] The dislike was mutual, and let's not forget that Charlotte had prevented the marriage of her own brother and Caroline once upon a time. Though the women didn't see eye to eye, George and Augusta corresponded throughout the marital feuding of the Prince and Princess of Wales. Augusta encouraged her brother to stand by Caroline as the wronged party, and at first, that was exactly what he did. Once Caroline's scandalous behaviour got too much for the king, his fondness cooled into a dutiful civility.

Duchess Augusta was widowed after her husband succumbed to injuries sustained on the battlefield. She had never truly settled on the continent and had belligerently maintained her British traditions over the decades, so, with little left to detain her in Europe, she headed home to England. Once upon a time, Augusta had reluctantly guided the bewildered young Charlotte through her first hours at the English court, but now, nearly fifty years later, Augusta was to return as a guest in Charlotte's domain.

Charlotte welcomed her sister-in-law back with a splendid dinner and it seemed as though all the bad blood had been forgotten. After all, it was a long time since Augusta had carped about Charlotte to Lord Malmesbury, when he had arrived in Brunswick to accompany Caroline of Brunswick to England and her husband-to-be. Nor was Charlotte a timid, wide-eyed young princess anymore. She had been through the wringer, and faced trials that she had never even dreamed of. Augusta was as opinionated as ever, but this time there could no doubt who held sway over the British court.

Act Three

Guardian

Engraven On My Heart

As the king neared his Jubilee on 25 October 1809, his health grew ever more perilous. Virtually blind, crippled by rheumatism, and often in a state of confusion, he played a small role in the celebrations but left the public appearances to his wife and daughters. Charlotte hosted a pageant at Frogmore for 1,000 ticketholders, who witnessed a breath-taking display of fireworks, music, and performance. But her husband's absence pricked at her.

Also absent was Princess Amelia, whose health had continued to decline. Instead, she remained confined at Windsor, cared for by her sisters and becoming slowly but surely more frustrated with her lot. Amelia had once been robust and healthy, a keen horsewoman with a zest for life, but now she was confined to her bed. As her health grew weaker, she clung hopelessly to the possibility of marriage to Charles FitzRoy. She practised signing herself as AFR, in honour of FitzRoy, but the chance of marriage was so remote as to be non-existent. To take the request to the king was something that Charlotte would never do.

The year had started with a fire that ravaged Charlotte's apartments in St James's, and it had gone downhill from there. Queen Charlotte was well aware of how much her husband adored Amelia and how damaging her death would be to his mental health. Emily, as he called her, was his unabashed favourite, the baby of the family, and the only one who seemed to truly understand him. Amelia visited her father daily despite her infirmity, and they took dinner at a table set for two, sharing secret jokes and stories to which no one else was privy. Charlotte, on the other hand, no longer travelled alone with her husband and insisted on having one of their daughters present should she visit him. The very idea of her taking private dinners with George had long since fallen by the wayside.

Under the terms of the Royal Marriages Act, once Amelia reached 25 she could make a request to the Privy Council for permission to wed, but in the event, she was far too ill to do so. She wrote sadly to FitzRoy, complaining that Princess Mary watched her like a hawk and confiding her worry that 'to get rid of me is [Queen Charlotte's] object on every account.' It goes without saying that Charlotte didn't want to get rid of her daughter, whilst Mary was always Amelia's devoted and loving nurse. But all Amelia wanted was FitzRoy.

In 1807, gossip spread through the royal household that Amelia claimed the queen had 'sanctioned the promise of a marriage the moment the K[ing] was dead.' There were some things that Charlotte was willing to let go, but in mentioning the king's death, this had crossed a line. Charlotte was filled with rage and tore Amelia's attendants off a strip, whilst telling Amelia that her behaviour had to change, before it had catastrophic consequences for her father.

Charlotte believed that Amelia's friend and attendant, Theresa Villiers, lay at the root of the gossip. Mrs Villiers loved being at the centre of drama and she encouraged Amelia's complaints against the queen and her hopeless adoration of FitzRoy. Indeed, when Amelia wanted to see a copy of the Royal Marriages Act, it was Mrs Villiers to whom she entrusted the task. In an effort to keep the two apart, Charlotte sent Amelia to Weymouth to take the sea air in 1809. Far from wanting to be rid of her youngest child, the queen was anxious for Amelia's worsening health.

'I have no imaginary fears about dear Amelia,' she wrote to Lady George Murray. 'Though her weak state of health, and sufferings whenever she travels, make me expect the worse; but when I think of the alteration for the better before she left us, I look forward to have at least as good, if not better news of her, when she has passed some quiet days.'[1] To the contrary, Amelia wrote ever more furious letters to Wales, in which she blamed her mother for her every woe. One shouldn't rush to judge the young princess, though. She was dying, and every treatment she was now subjected to was more painful than the last.

Isolated and brooding, Amelia languished in bed with precious few visits from the mother she resented so much. Against Amelia's wishes, Charlotte entrusted her care to Sir Francis Milman and Sir Henry Halford, who subjected her to cupping and bleeding before turning to the use of seatons, hoping they would offer Amelia some respite from the pain and inflammation in her breast. Seatons were silken tubes that were inserted through holes cut into the patient's body, through which fluids would then be drawn. In Amelia's case they became embedded in the skin and her maid, Mary Gaskoin, had to apply caustic to her flesh to burn them out. Mrs Villiers urged Amelia to seek a second opinion and, after lobbying Charlotte, Dr Robert Pope was permitted to join the team. All his presence did was inflate the number of doctors around the princess's bedside, each less able to help her than the last.

Amelia knew that she was wasting away, and she mourned for the life that she would never live. Confined to her bed and nursed by Mary, she brooded on what would become of FitzRoy after her death. For ten years she had loved the equerry and now, in her final months, Amelia was determined to leave him with something to remember her by. She prepared a will in which she left FitzRoy virtually everything she possessed in the world. In it, she told him to leave court and start a new life, where she would be at his side in spirit.

By the spring of 1810, Amelia's days were growing short. Nothing brought her any respite and her symptoms were now unmistakably those of tuberculosis. The king and queen visited her bedside daily, but the person she trusted with her deepest secrets was the Prince of Wales. It was with him that Amelia shared all her hopes and fears, and to him that she confided her undying love of Charles FitzRoy. As she grew weaker, Princess Amelia's doctors told her parents that they should prepare for the worst. Their youngest daughter was dying.

As the health of the princess declined, so too did that of her father. Though the matter of the Regency had been discussed previously, this time all concerned knew that it was no longer a question of if, but when. When George suffered a paroxysm in the last days of Amelia's life, his physician, Dr Matthew Baillie, declared that this, coupled with a certain frantic excitement in his demeanour, was a sure sign that his madness was returning. Once again, George was isolated from his wife, and Charlotte wrote a heartfelt letter to the man she already knew she had lost:

> My dearest King. Dr John Willis has made me very happy by putting into my Hands Your very Affectionnate Letter which contains Your approbation of my Conduct which both my Inclination & Duty led me to fullfill & which will never cease but with my Life. Our Separation must be & really is equally painfull to us both & happy as it would make me & Your Children to come & see You, The Physicians assure me that such a meeting ought not to take place at present & therefore am under the painfull Necessity to deprive myself of so Satisfactory a pleasure which would prove a happiness to Your truely [sic] attached Wife Charlotte.[2]

Every day, multiple bulletins on Amelia's condition were read out to the virtually blind king, who interrogated their contents for any sign of a miracle. Each afternoon, he was helped from his rooms and to Amelia's bedside, where he sat for hours. Sometimes he was silent, sometimes he wept, and sometimes, when both father and daughter were feeling able, they conversed on matters of faith, taking solace in their shared company.

Painfully aware that she had little time left, Amelia commissioned a mourning ring for her father. Decorated with diamonds and containing a lock of her hair, the ring was inscribed with Amelia's name and the simple request, *remember me*. The ring was made up as a matter of urgency and despite Princess Mary's pleas to think of the king's nerves, Amelia was steadfast in her determination to give it to him herself. When Amelia slid the ring onto her sightless father's finger, she asked him to promise that he would never forget her. Through his sobs, he assured his daughter, 'That I can never do, you are engraven on my heart.'

Amelia had planned no such gift for her mother, but George became so distressed that she was forced to relent. To the woman she blamed for all her woes, she left a locket containing a lock of her own hair. It was merely a gesture to salve the distress of the father she so adored.

> DEATH of the PRINCESS AMELIA – We have the painful duty to announce the Death of the Princess Amelia, whose affliction has so long excited the lively interest of the public – not merely from her own most amiable qualities, but from the sympathy which they felt in the sufferings of her affectionate parents. She died yesterday noon, and without any pain. She was so totally exhausted by decay, as to make it almost impossible to tell when life was really extinguished.[3]

On 2 November 1810, Princess Amelia died. Her last words were, 'Tell Charles I die blessing him.' Queen Charlotte was summoned to Augusta Lodge to view the body of her daughter, which lay wasted and lifeless beneath her bedclothes. As the princess was prepared for burial, Charlotte retreated to the company of her attendants to mourn, but for the king the consequences were far greater.

Although it was clear that George III was no longer well enough to reign, the death of Amelia was the final straw. Though some hopeful voices in the press actually wondered if the knowledge that Amelia was no longer suffering might help the king to recover, such a miracle was never on the horizon. Instead, the loss of his favourite child tipped George headfirst into a madness from which he would never emerge. The day after Amelia's death, George was straitjacketed. Within the week, the Cabinet had imposed a visit by Dr Robert Willis, despite the resistance of all the royal family.

From this point on, protecting her husband became Queen Charlotte's mission. She and Lady Harcourt were rarely apart as Charlotte mourned, but when her husband began to ask what had become of Amelia's will, the queen panicked. She feared that if George learned that Amelia had left everything to FitzRoy, it would only make his condition worse. Charlotte asked the Prince of Wales and the Duke of Cambridge, Amelia's executors, to deal with the possibly embarrassing will, and with FitzRoy's agreement, it was decided that they would be officially named as the sole beneficiaries. Though they assured him that all her dying wishes would be obeyed, this wasn't the case.

Instead, the princes rode roughshod over their sister's will and even though FitzRoy made no claims on her estate – not even to reclaim £5,000 he had loaned her – Wales and Cambridge made no effort to treat him with sensitivity. They eventually gave him a few books and pieces of plate and FitzRoy, embattled by grief, let the matter rest.[4]

The Care and Custody of His Majesty

> It appeared to [the House] that the Prince of Wales ought unquestionably to be appointed Regent, to exercise the powers of Government in the name and on behalf of his Majesty during his illness. In the second place, it was his opinion, that generally all the powers of Government should be conveyed into his Royal Highness's hands. The next provision of the measure was, that her Majesty should be continued guardian of his Majesty's person; that to her Majesty should be intrusted the care and custody of his Majesty. There was also to be a provision containing due and necessary precautions for the notification of his Majesty's recovery whenever it should happen, and for securing to him the resumption of his royal power on such recovery. He did not mean to propose any limit to the duration of the Regency, but [considering] the evidence of the Physicians … as well as the historical information respecting the former attacks to which his Majesty had been exposed, they would be justified in contemplating his Majesty's recovery to a very distant period.[5]

One matter that couldn't rest was that of the Regency. Dr Robert Willis pulled no punches when asked for his verdict on his patient. He attributed the monarch's perilous condition to shock at the death of Amelia, and admitted that there had been moments when he feared for George's life. The violence of the attacks increased with each new relapse, he confirmed, and there was no immediate recovery on the cards. With this in mind, he requested that his brother, John, join him in caring for the king. Charlotte dreaded her husband's wrath should he regain his wits and discover that the doctors Willis had been tending him. 'How Cutting it is to my feeling to do that which if the King recovers may perhaps forever make me forfeit His good oppinion [sic],' she admitted to her eldest son. 'My conscience is clear, for I have kept off the attendance of [John Willis] above a year [and am] yielding with the greatest reluctance & almost with a broken heart.'[6]

In Parliament, Spencer Perceval drew up the fundamentals of the Bill on the last day of 1810. Among the provisions was one that ruled Queen Charlotte would be responsible for the care of the king's person and for appointments in the royal household. She would be assisted in her role by a Queen's Council consisting of eight privy councillors, headed by the Archbishops of York and Canterbury. The council would receive bulletins on the king's condition and had the ultimate authority to declare him sane and return him to power. However, to those who opposed the measure, this went far beyond care for the king's person.

In handing this resolution to Charlotte, Perceval had also handed her a level of political power that she had never before wielded. Should she wish, Charlotte now had a say in who should hold over a dozen great offices of state and if the Prince of Wales went the way his friends were hoping and replaced his father's Tory administration with a Whig one, then she could frustrate his efforts enormously. Yet Charlotte had never sought political power and still hoped that her husband might one day recover, though she knew now that such hopes were slight. She let Wales know that the king was lucid and had been pleased to receive Perceval's assurances that for now at least, the ship was stable.

In fact, when the moment came, the new Prince Regent chose to maintain the status quo. On 4 February 1811, he wrote that 'the Prince feels it incumbent upon him, at this precise juncture, to communicate to Mr. Perceval his intention not to remove from their stations those whom he finds there, as his Majesty's official servants.'[7] To put it simply, he did not dismiss the administration his father had appointed, electing instead to continue with Perceval's government.[8] The hopes of the Whigs had been dashed due to the prince's 'dread that any act of the Regent might in the smallest degree have the effect of interfering with his Sovereign's recovery.'[9]

The Prince Regent's handling of the situation was a great comfort to Charlotte, and she finally came to believe that he would govern in his father's interest, rather than his own. She held regular audiences with the members of the council and immediately after the Regent decided to retain the ongoing administration, was pleased to report that George 'seems not to be so much fallen away as I expected.'[10] In fact, she felt so well that she was even able to provide the council with gentle entertainment after the meeting had broken up. Yet whilst Charlotte's relationship with her son was more solid than ever, her relationship with her daughters was anything but. The princesses were little girls no longer. They wanted a taste of freedom.

Take a Mother's Advice

The Prince Regent understood the frustrations of his cosseted sisters, trapped in the home Princess Sophia had nicknamed 'the nunnery', and he wanted to help them if he could. He gave each of his unmarried sisters a pension of £7,900, liveries, carriages, and eventually even residences, and promised that he would make a case to the queen for letting them have a little more freedom. Perhaps, he ventured, they could serve as chaperones to his teenage daughter, Charlotte. This way they would be able to mix in society under the guise of duty.

Charlotte saw through the ploy straight away. They might be grown women, but as far as the queen was concerned, any suggestion that they were enjoying life was an affront to good morals and an insult to their father. She denied them the permission to be present in any house with an unmarried man – including their own brothers – without a chaperone present and claimed that the very thought of them seeking to go into society had left her so distressed that she could barely stand it. Queen Charlotte, who had never 'felt as shattered in my life',[11] withdrew into melodramatic self-pity.

> [The princesses must] take a mothers [sic] advice. Let me beseech you well to Consider that your situation is very different to that of your Brothers, who by their Situations in life must appear in Public, and have their Duties to perform in which they would injure themselves if they were not to appear. But in your Sex, and under the present Melancholy Situation of your father the going to Public Amusements except where Duty calls you would be the highest mark of indecency possible. [With] every step any one of you intends to take, always to keep in remembrance that no age whatever is excepted from being criticized, and that the higher the character, the more will it be traduced.[12]

'Poor old wretches as we are, four old cats, four old wretches, a dead weight upon you, old lumber to the country, like old clothes,' Princess Sophia wrote to the Regent, ably summing up the frustration and unhappiness she and her sisters felt. 'I wonder you do not vote for putting us in a sack and drowning us in the Thames. Two of us would be fine food for the fishes and as to Minny and me, we will take our chance together.'

But not all the princesses were willing to submit to the queen's dominance. Like Princess Amelia, the spirited Princess Augusta also had a secret. She had been in love with equerry Brent Spencer for years, and with her brother now Regent, it was he who had to give permission for the wedding. The king and queen's consent was no longer necessary. 'We have neither Health or Spirits to support for any length of time ... the Treatment which we have experienced whenever any Proposal has been made for Our absenting Ourselves for a few days from the Queen's Roof,'[13] she told him on behalf of the princesses, and she had reached her limit.

I now beseech you, my Dearest, to consider our situation. If it is in your power to make us happy I know you will. I am sensible that should you agree to our Union it can *only* proceed from your affection for me, and your desire of promoting my happiness and that of a Worthy Man. It is not a fancy taken up vaguely, our acquaintance having existed for twelve years, and our attachment been *mutually acknowledged nine years ago*. To you we look up, for our future comfort and peace of mind. Your sanction is what we aspire to! ...

Should your Answer be favourable to my Heart's Dearest and nearest wish, I shall beg of you to have the goodness to name it to the Queen. No consideration in the world (even certain of all that is *essential, Your Permission*) shall make me take such a step unknown to Her. I owe it to Her as my Mother, though I am too honest to affect asking for *Her consent, as it is not necessary*. Nor shall the most Anxious wish of my Heart ever make me unjust or unreasonable. I am certain the Queen cannot approve if She merely thinks of my birth and station. But that is the *only reason* She can object to it, and I shall never blame Her for it. But when she considers the Character of the Man, the faithfulness and length of our attachment, and the struggles that I have been compelled to make, never retracting from any of my Duties, though suffering

Martyrdom from anxiety of *Mind* and *deprivation of happiness*, I am sure that She will say long and great has been my trial, and correct has been my Conduct.[14]

It's heart-breaking to think of Augusta, by now a woman in her mid-forties, desperately hoping for the approval from her mother that would never come. Though it's perfectly possible that the Regent granted a secret marriage for Augusta and Spencer, who enjoyed a glittering career in the royal household after 1812, it was not one that Charlotte would have approved of.

Yet perhaps we should reserve judgement on the queen until we have considered her own trials. She had been steadfast beside her husband, endured his insults and his attacks, both physical and psychological, until the man she loved had all but disappeared, his personality changed beyond recognition. She in turn had lost her carefree optimism and her love of life, and had developed a suspicious nature and a domineering temper.

The king knew little of the comings and goings of his family and Charlotte, who had become more and more exasperated with him, no longer had the patience to revisit such matters. After years of tolerating her husband's declarations of love for Lady Pembroke, even his claims that he had secretly married her no longer upset the queen. She had become immune to the constant assault on her feelings and had hardened her carapace until she no longer fled in tears from the man she had married. Even when he was lucid, her patience towards George was so thin that Princess Elizabeth, who sadly admitted that 'I find my mother much altered', actually asked Henry Halford if he would intervene and speak to her about being more understanding. Yet one must be sympathetic to Charlotte too. Her husband increasingly didn't even recognise her, but she remembered every single thing that had passed between them – for better or worse.

After June 1812, Queen Charlotte never visited the king again, and as Prinny (the nickname by which the capricious Prince Regent had become known) tried to smooth the road to independent homes for his sisters, the queen insisted that she too should have her own establishment. In her mind, she was now alone.

The Regent couldn't talk his mother into okaying Augusta's dreams of marriage, but he did manage to bring her round on the question of a chaperone. Princess Charlotte of Wales was entering into society, Prinny pointed out, and who better to be at her side than her morally upstanding aunts, who had been so well brought up by the queen? Though she initially resisted such ideas, when Charlotte finally agreed, Princess Mary was determined to make a go of this unexpected opportunity. She went on a shopping spree, filling her rooms with new dresses that were an absolute necessity if she was going to accompany the young and fashionable Princess Charlotte in society.

If Prinny thought that his mother had thawed, he had badly misjudged the situation. Thinking that the argument had passed, he invited the princesses to accompany their young charge to the State Opening of Parliament. Charlotte had other ideas. She flatly denied them permission to attend and even wrote to the Prince Regent, ably assuming the role of victim:

> Can there be, I appeal to your own feelings, a more painful, a more horrible situation, than the one your father labours under? And it was not my duty to state to your sisters, that they having no personal duty which calls upon their presence at the House of Lords, it would show more attention to female delicacy to decline it, but left it to their option to do as they please.[15]

This time, Mary and Elizabeth followed their hearts. When they returned to Windsor after attending the State Opening, a violent argument shook the castle walls. Her daughters were immoral, disloyal, and cared not a jot for their father, Charlotte spat, but this time Mary and Elizabeth spat back. In the heat of the argument, Elizabeth slammed her fist into a Bible, and Mary declared that she would no longer submit to the lash of her mother's temper. Queen Charlotte was losing her stranglehold on the tightknit group that had sustained her through her trials. Ironically, it was probably this that saved her relationship with the very daughters she sought to control. After all, no family escapes its share of arguments and perhaps, once she realised that her temper and her penchant for martyrdom would only drive them away, Queen Charlotte let nature take its course.

There is no greater proof of this change in the household dynamic than the fact that, when William Frederick, Duke of Gloucester, came calling for the hand of Princess Mary in 1816, his request was granted. The nunnery was opening up at last.

Exposing Herself Like an Opera Girl

The Dowager Duchess of Brunswick, who told Lord Malmesbury in 1793 that she would never return to England because, 'twenty years absence and thirty years living with the Queen, had made [George III] forget her,'[16] did just that after the conquering of her marital lands. With time and age having buffed off the rough edges of their relationship, she and Charlotte managed to reach a peaceful mutual existence before the Duchess died in 1813. In her later years, as the behaviour of her daughter, Caroline of Brunswick, became more scandalous, Charlotte grew sympathetic towards Augusta, and their old rancour faded into mutual tolerance. The king knew nothing of her passing, but the queen saw to it that her sister-in-law was buried with due ceremony in the vault at Windsor. The year after her mother's death, the troublesome Princess of Wales finally left England to kick up her heels on the continent.

In 1814, Ernest, Duke of Cumberland, proposed to his cousin, Duchess Frederica of Mecklenburg-Strelitz. Cumberland was no stranger to gossip, having been implicated in the bizarre suicide of his valet, and his prospective bride had known her fair share of scandal too. One might wonder how a love match, such as that between Cumberland and Frederica, might have attracted controversy, but it did. Frederica, who was the daughter of Charlotte's brother, Charles II, had already been married twice. She had also been engaged to one of Cumberland's brothers. Her first marriage, to Prince Frederick Louis Charles of Prussia, ended in widowhood just three years after the wedding, amid rumours of affairs on both sides. The year after she was widowed, she entered into an unofficial engagement with Charlotte and George's son, Prince Adolphus, Duke of Cambridge. Cambridge had sought the permission of George III, who asked him to wait until the war with France had ended to make a proposal. Eventually that relationship collapsed too, with Charlotte sure that Frederica had abandoned her son for another.

In 1798, less than two years after she was widowed, Frederica fell pregnant by Prince Frederick William of Solms-Braunfels. The couple were quickly married but their child died in infancy. The dissolute Prince Frederick William resumed his old lifestyle and the couple separated, though they were still officially husband and wife when Frederica and Cumberland met in 1813. Frederica's husband agreed to her request for a divorce, only to die with suspicious haste. The finger of blame was pointed at his widow, who was suspected of murdering her unwanted husband with poison. Charlotte thought that it would be for the best if her niece didn't remarry, but she had set her sights on Cumberland and he was happy to reciprocate.

It seemed to be a year for weddings. As Cumberland applied to Prinny for permission to marry, Charlotte's granddaughter, Princess Charlotte of Wales, was also planning a wedding. Her groom-to-be was William, the Hereditary Prince of Orange, and

Queen Charlotte viewed both prospective marriages with doubt. She suspected that Princess Charlotte had accepted her father's choice of Orange simply to be able to strike out on her own, whilst she really didn't like the idea of Cumberland becoming the third husband of a woman who seemed to attract trouble. In the case of Princess Charlotte and Prince William, she was quite right, and the marriage was eventually called off by the bride in favour of a love match to Prince Leopold of Saxe-Coburg-Saalfeld.

George III had always disapproved of marriages between cousins, even though he had sanctioned them in his time. The collapse of the union between the Regent and Caroline of Brunswick had done nothing to convince him that he was wrong, but the decision was no longer his to make. Charlotte's hurricane temper was still one to be reckoned with, but she had always been more severe with her daughters than her sons. Though she advised the Duke of Cumberland that he shouldn't make any marriage plans until his bride-to-be had mourned for her late husband, he was spared her ire.

Embarrassingly, despite the Regent's request to his government that they give Cumberland a generous allowance on the occasion of his marriage, they refused to do so on account of his unpopularity in the United Kingdom. Although Charlotte had given her permission for the wedding, she didn't want to receive the couple in England until what she considered a suitable period of mourning had passed. With that in mind, it was agreed that they would marry in Germany before travelling to the UK for a second marriage.

All of this was moving far too slowly for Cumberland, who was keen to get the ring on his new bride's finger. As he waited for an English cleric to arrive, he wondered what the delay was. The queen's brother also wondered what was causing the hold-up, as he was keen to have his daughter married and on her way once more. Charlotte consoled them with assurances that the unavoidable delays were due to the political situation in Europe rather than any deliberate prevarication. After all, she had hardly anticipated Napoleon's escape from Elba when she gave her blessing to the marriage.

Eventually, the deed was done, and Charlotte hoped that would be an end to it. She had decided on reflection that she would not receive Cumberland's bride at all, believing that if she did, the rabble-rousing Princess of Wales might find some way to make capital of her visit. Cumberland arrived in England alone and made it his business to change his mother's mind. For this, he enlisted the help of the Prince Regent, but Charlotte wouldn't budge.

All of this provided rich pickings for the opposition when Cumberland lodged a request for increased financial support with the House of Commons. His request was denied by one solitary vote. However, the matter of Cumberland's marriage wasn't only one for family: there was the line of succession to consider. Despite a legion of illegitimate offspring, the fifteen royal children had managed to produce only one legitimate grandchild between them. That was Princess Charlotte who, as a woman, was exempt from succeeding to the throne of Hanover. Eventually, Cumberland would become the King of Hanover when Queen Victoria succeeded to the British throne.

With his defeat in Parliament still fresh, Cumberland set out to join his bride on the continent, armed with Prinny's suggestion that he and Frederica should solemnise their marriage in England as soon as possible. Despite the queen's resistance, the couple arrived at Dover in the last days of August and their marriage was solemnised at Carlton House in a ceremony conducted by the Archbishop of Canterbury. Still Charlotte wouldn't back down and receive her niece, who was now also her daughter-in-law. Even a personal visit by Charlotte's nephew, George, Hereditary Grand Duke of Mecklenburg-Strelitz, did nothing to mollify the queen. Though she spoke kindly of the new princess, the Hereditary Grand Duke's pleas to receive his sister fell on deaf ears.

Charlotte's own children knew that there was a point at which one had to admit defeat, but Hereditary Grand Duke George had no idea how to handle his aunt. Immediately after their audience, he wrote her a letter in which he restated the cause of his sister, Charlotte's new daughter-in-law. It was like lighting the touch paper on a firework. Charlotte took his letter as a personal insult and accused him of bullying and intimidation. Insulted, angry, and morally indignant, she banished him from her presence. She would not see him again.

What is most unexpected about this is the fact that Charlotte never subjected Cumberland to one of her rages. She was motivated partly by concern for her granddaughter, Princess Charlotte of Wales, whom she feared might somehow be sucked into the drama if she was allowed to mix with her scandalous new aunt. The queen adored the young lady and saw in her the next hope of the royal family, if only she could be encouraged not to follow the example of her mother, who was busy 'exposing herself like an opera girl'.[17] When Princess Charlotte eventually asked to be freed from her unwanted engagement to the Prince of Orange, the queen ruefully supported her. Her own marriage of duty had become one of love, and she hoped that one day her granddaughter might enjoy the same.

An Unpleasant and Painful Business

The marriage of the Prince and Princess of Wales had been an unmitigated disaster. That it had somehow managed to produce a child should be considered as something of a minor miracle, and once the couple separated, there was to be no reconciliation. The Delicate Investigation of 1806 had seen Caroline of Brunswick's behaviour investigated amid claims of an illegitimate child and, though she was found innocent on that charge, questions of adultery were never fully dismissed. Of course, Caroline certainly did have a very rich sex life, just as her estranged husband did, but it was he who held the power, not his wife. The fate of their daughter, Charlotte, had been to become caught between the pair, pulled this way and that with the king in the middle, constantly trying to steady the ship. Her parents loved her, it's true, but it's also true that she was the biggest weapon they had against each other. They battled for custody, for the rights to manage her education and, of course, for influence over who she would marry.

It seemed as though the Prince Regent had won that particular battle. He had done his best to control his daughter, packing her off in her early years to live in Montague House with her governesses whilst he entertained his mistresses. She and her mother met in secret thanks to the princess's sympathetic attendants, but as Charlotte grew, there were indications that she'd inherited her mother's free spirit. Charlotte was the perfect granddaughter when she took trips to the seaside or strolled in the royal gardens with her grandmother, but there was another, more dramatic side to the young lady. Princess Charlotte was determined to make her presence felt, and her father was horrified by reports of her leaning out of her opera box to blow kisses to the Regent's former Whig friends, now his sworn opponents.

In response, the Prince Regent tightened the screws still further, with a concerned Queen Charlotte behind him every step of the way. She was pleased to learn 'of the very Judicious and Prudent manner in which the princes Confidential Servants have advised Him to act upon this very unpleasant & Painfull Business.' Gone was the flighty, troublesome eldest son, replaced by a responsible father, who led Charlotte to 'rejoice much that the Prince has spoke Himself to His daughter & am Delighted at the propriety & Feeling of Her Conduct.'[18]

In order to bring his daughter into line once and for all, Prinny decided that she would be married to William, Prince of Orange.

Given how badly his own arranged marriage has gone, it might come as a surprise that the Regent was willing to subject his only child to the same fate, but making a good royal match was all that was on his mind.

When Queen Charlotte learned of the intended marriage, she wrote to her son to offer her congratulations. She was far from effusive.

> My dearest Son.
> Your Kindness of charging the Duke of York with the Commission of acquainting me with the intended Alliance between Your Daughter & the Hereditary Prince of Orange calls for my most gratefull [sic] acknowledgement. My Congratulations upon this Event. You will not doubt to be Sincere when I say, may this Union prove to be as Happy as Your own hath been Fatal.[19]

Though Princess Charlotte had been willing to go along with the marriage at first, that changed when she met the cash-strapped Prince Leopold of Saxe-Coburg-Saalfeld at a party. Now she saw the prospect of a marriage not for duty, but love, but when she asked Prinny to release her from her promise, he wouldn't hear of it. The contracts had been signed and, suspecting his daughter wouldn't take *no* for an answer, he made plans to send her to Windsor, where she would be secluded at Cranbourne Lodge. Here she wouldn't be able to cause any more trouble, and it would be a lot more difficult to see her errant mother too.

The public loved Caroline and young Charlotte as much as they loathed the Prince Regent, and they clamoured to know what right Prinny had to make his daughter miserable. As Queen Charlotte was on her way to a Drawing Room, a mob waylaid her chair, hammering on the glass and demanding that she answer for her son's actions. The doughty queen lowered the glass and told them, 'I am above seventy years of age, I have been more than fifty years Queen of England, and I never was hissed by a mob before.' Chastened, the crowd backed away and the chair proceeded on its way. When the time came for her to make her return journey, Prinny insisted she take extra guards, but Charlotte refused. If he tried to force bodyguards on her, she told him, she would walk home alone instead.

Princess Charlotte was just as fearless as her namesake. When she learned of her proposed move to Cranbourne Lodge, she fled from the Regent's home and raced out into the street. There she commandeered a cab to take her to her mother, where she intended to remain until the marriage to Orange was called off. Instead, Caroline's Whig advisors convinced Princess Charlotte that she must return to her father's custody, pointing out that it would be Caroline who faced censure, not Charlotte.

Charlotte's flight gave her father a fright and he agreed to listen to her concerns. She was the darling of the public and the last thing he wanted was to attract even more criticism from his subjects. When Princess Caroline threw her weight behind her daughter's plea, that did it. Prinny dared not be seen to be forcing Charlotte into a marriage that she was so vehemently opposed to, and he agreed to call off the wedding and meet Prince Leopold, though he made no promises that he'd welcome another proposal. Happily, the two princes got on like a house on fire and Princess Charlotte got her way. Satisfied that her daughter was settled, the Princess of Wales could finally leave England to indulge in some scandals of her own.

Though it went against all her beliefs regarding propriety to call off an engagement, Queen Charlotte stilled her tongue. After the years of turmoil that had followed her eldest son's marriage, perhaps she had come to realise that a degree of marital love might do no harm in the long term. Returning from a trip to the south coast with Princess Charlotte and her daughters, the queen was sure that nothing would make her granddaughter happier than a marriage to Prince Leopold, and she lent her support to the match.

Queen Charlotte was a vital part of the marriage arrangements, advising her young namesake on matters of dress and her trousseau. Nobody was more proud than Charlotte when she attended the wedding in the Crimson Room of Carlton House on 2 May 1816. Despite this, we shouldn't be deceived into thinking that the queen had entirely given up her love of protocol. The new bride had to firmly disavow her grandmother of any notion that she and her groom would start out on their honeymoon with a chaperone of the queen's choosing seated between them in their carriage.

The second royal wedding that year was less the stuff of romantic fiction than the first. Prince William Frederick, Duke of Gloucester and Edinburgh, known to some as 'Silly Billy', had always nursed hopes that he might one day marry Princess Charlotte of Wales. When that didn't come off, he set his sights on Princess Mary instead. Upon learning of his proposal from her brother, the Prince Regent, Mary needed time to consider whether marriage to the dull Duke was the price she was willing to pay for freedom. Having secured the would-be groom's promise that they would live close by and that Princess Mary would be able to visit her father whenever she wished, Charlotte gave no opposition to the match. Perhaps she knew that she had lost that particular battle.

The Duke of Gloucester and Princess Mary were married on 22 July 1816. It had taken decades, but she was finally free of the Windsor nunnery.

Scathed By the Hand of Heaven

Queen Charlotte, who had so far resisted every effort to separate her from her daughters, had finally begun to mellow. No longer fearful of her husband's next relapse, her sadness at his now permanent condition was tempered by the knowledge that he was, in some strange way, at peace. He was no longer assailed by the concerns of politics and government, and she no longer had to spend every moment scrutinising his behaviour for an indication that he was unwell. Every morning, Charlotte met with Dr John Willis, who shared the king's quarters at Windsor, and received an update on George's health. Though 'The Queen is the only person who is admitted to a discourse with the KING, except the medical gentlemen and his Majesty's personal attendants,'[20] to all intents and purposes, she had lost his companionship forever.

The year 1816 had seen a pair of royal weddings, but it ended with a tragedy. On 6 November 1816, Charlotte's brother, Grand Duke Charles, died. Queen Charlotte was bereft, and her depression only deepened when protests against the Prince Regent turned violent, and his carriage was attacked at Westminster. Her condition declined so much that her Drawing Rooms were cancelled and she retired for a time to the countryside as a guest of the Duke of Marlborough. The trip did much to restore the queen, but almost as soon as she returned to Windsor, she fell ill again. This time, Henry Halford prescribed a trip to take the waters at Bath, accompanied by Princess Elizabeth. Here they renewed their acquaintance with that old royal retainer, Frances Burney.

In Bath, Queen Charlotte seemed to recover her spirits. She received regular missives regarding the condition of Princess Charlotte, who was by now heavily pregnant, and awaited the arrival of her great-grandchild with anticipation. Yet when news came, it was the worst imaginable. Almost a year to the day after the Grand Duke's death, tragedy struck again. Princess Charlotte had struggled through an agonising labour to deliver a stillborn boy. She died soon afterwards, and her loss plunged the nation into mourning. Charlotte's happy reception at Bath was forgotten as she returned to the side of the Prince Regent at Windsor, but her carriage was heckled in the streets of the capital by a crowd convinced that the queen simply didn't care. In the past, she had lifted her chin and ordered the mob that surrounded her to back off, but this time she huddled back in fear.

By the time Queen Charlotte reached Windsor, she was distraught. The people might have thought that she was incapable of sadness, but they were wrong. Sadness had become a way of life for her. Queen Charlotte mourned for her late granddaughter and the agony of her loss left the Prince Regent almost mad with grief, but the public wanted somebody to blame. They demanded to know why no members of the royal family had been present at the birth or the moment of Princess Charlotte's death, with one newspaper decrying, 'We deplore only that she was not supported in the hour of trial by the tender relatives whom she was known to love.'[21]

This tabloid breast-beating did a disservice to the sadness of the queen and Prince Regent. Just as the death of Princess Amelia had proved a fateful moment in the decline of the king, so too did the death of Princess Charlotte have the same impact on the queen. Though she returned to Bath, it was a sickly, sad Charlotte who sought comfort in the waters. She was gradually fading away.

Perhaps it was Charlotte's awareness of her own mortality that caused her odd reaction to a proposal from Frederick, Hereditary Prince of Hesse-Homburg, for the hand of Princess Elizabeth. Years earlier, he had expressed an interest in Augusta which had been rebuffed, and his latest offer came entirely out of the blue. Though Princess Mary had been in two minds over her own nuptials, Elizabeth had no such reservations. With a youthful enthusiasm at odds with her years, she excitedly told her sisters and her mother that she wished to accept.

The Prince Regent needed no convincing, but despite Charlotte's acquiescence to Mary's marriage, the queen was not quite so pleased for Elizabeth. Elizabeth had been her most constant companion over the years, but now she was champing at the bit to marry and start a new life on the continent. Queen Charlotte took it as a personal affront, but Prinny was able to convince his mother to give her reluctant, tearful blessing.

The couple were married on 7 April 1818, and at the festivities that followed nobody was more welcoming than Queen Charlotte. Richard Rush, the United States Minister to the United Kingdom, captured the scene sensitively in his memoirs. Charlotte, it seemed, could still put on a show.

> The whole demeanour of the Queen was remarkable. This venerable personage, the head of a large family, her children at that moment clustering about her; the female head of a great empire – in the seventy-sixth year of her age – went the rounds of her company, speaking to all; no one did she omit. There was a kindliness in her manner, from which time had struck away useless forms. Around her neck hung a miniature portrait of the king. He was absent – scathed by the hand of heaven; a marriage going on in one of his palaces – he, the lonely, suffering tenant of another. But the portrait was a token superior to a crown! It bespoke the natural glory of wife and mother, eclipsing the artificial glory of Queen. For more than fifty years this royal pair had lived together in affection. The scene would have been one of interest in any class of life. May it not be noticed on a throne?[22]

When the newlyweds left for Hesse-Homburg, they promised Queen Charlotte that they would return within the year. At the time, nobody knew that the queen would not live to receive them.

A Strange and Unaccountable Dread

Queen Charlotte made her final public appearances in April 1818. She held her traditional St George's Day Drawing Room and, on 29 April, visited the Mansion House for a prizegiving ceremony in honour of the National Society for Promoting the Education of the Poor. Here she made a donation of £500 and spoke with the celebrated reformer, Elizabeth Fry. With the queen's health in decline, her physicians were in near constant attendance to try to offer some respite from the spasms that she had begun to experience. The march of time could not be ignored, and familiar faces were dwindling as her daughters married and her loyal retainers retired or died. Each fresh goodbye was a reminder of the queen's advancing age.

By the time the Duke of Cambridge and Princess Augusta of Hesse-Kassel were married in the queen's London Drawing Room in June 1818, Charlotte was no longer well enough to undertake any public duties. Aware that her days were growing short, she became determined to return to her husband's side at Windsor, but Sir Henry Halford would not hear of it. Her health was simply too fragile to bear the journey. Halford suggested that she travel to Kew instead, where she could rest before hopefully continuing on to Windsor. Charlotte had not seen the king for an age, and she was seized by an urgent need to be by his side one last time. The fact that her own health prevented her from doing so plunged her into misery.

As she languished at Kew, Queen Charlotte knew that her travels were over. She would not be able to journey on to Windsor. Instead, the weddings of the Dukes of Kent and Clarence came to Kew. The dukes married Princess Victoria of Leiningen and Princess Adelaide of Saxe-Meiningen respectively in the presence of the queen on 11 July 1818. The Duke of Cumberland took no part in the celebrations. Queen Charlotte refused to receive his bride to the end and, bitter at her final rejection, the couple had left England for Europe just days earlier.

The queen who had once sat at the centre of her husband's world was now a fading relic of a bygone age. She was all too aware of her own mortality too, causing prime minister, Lord Liverpool, to reflect on her 'strange and unaccountable dread of everything that pertains to Death'.[23] Perhaps she sensed that its shadow was stalking ever longer. Despite being organised to a fault when it came to the management of her household, or the care of her husband and children, Charlotte's own affairs remained in disarray. She had made no arrangements for her estate after her death, and seemed determined not to do so.

> HER MAJESTY is also said to suffer extreme mental anxiety at her increasing inability to remove to Windsor, and regrets that she did not sooner follow the dictates of her feelings; for, in her present state, the journey, it seems, is deemed altogether impossible.[24]

At Windsor, the king played a tuneless melody on his harpsichord and spent long hours chatting to the phantoms of his dead sons, or inspecting troops that only he could see, whilst at Kew Charlotte's days were quiet. Her legs had swollen agonisingly, and she could no longer walk in the grounds that she adored, nor visit the menagerie that she had so lovingly established. Instead, she watched from her window, tended by her ladies and children as her condition grew weaker. Her chair was fitted with rollers so that she could be wheeled through her apartment, but by the second week of September, the very slightest movement was agony. Queen Charlotte was confined to her bedroom instead. Her children were advised not to stray too far from Kew, as it would soon be time to say a final goodbye.

With Princess Mary and Princess Augusta a constant presence at her bedside, Charlotte succumbed to the agonies of dropsy. Known today as oedema, dropsy is a swelling in the soft tissue caused by an excess of water, and is often a symptom of a more serious disorder. Even when she could no longer sit straight, but was bent to the right, the queen still refused to admit that her trip to Windsor was an impossibility. Instead, as the days drew on, she talked of little else.

In November 1818, the queen's condition took a sudden turn for the worse with a diagnosis of pneumonia. For days, the newspapers had printed bulletins of Queen Charlotte's health, by turns optimistic and fatalistic. Days before her death, the *Hampshire Telegraph and Sussex Chronicle etc.* concluded sadly, 'Her Majesty declines rapidly.'[25] The flesh of one of the queen's legs became so swollen by dropsy that it split open, turning gangrenous within days. Nothing further could be done, and the focus of the doctors shifted onto palliative medicine. Finally faced with the inevitable, Queen Charlotte signed her will with a weak, shaky signature before she slipped into sleep. The medical bulletins had never been exactly promising, but the doctors' final dispatch left no room for doubt.

> The Queen's state, last night, was one of great and imminent danger. Her MAJESTY continues very ill this morning.
>
> FR. MILMAN
>
> HENRY HALFORD

Yet for a woman who had feared death, at the end Charlotte was serene. No longer complaining of any pain, Queen Charlotte lay peaceful as she entered her final hours. She was surrounded by those who loved her, and Princess Mary and Princess Augusta were joined in their vigil by the Duke of York and the Prince Regent, who took his mother's hand and held it as she slipped away.

> This day, at one o'clock, the QUEEN departed this life, to the inexpressible grief of all the Royal Family, after a tedious illness, which her MAJESTY bore with the most pious fortitude and resignation. The many great and exemplary virtues, which so eminently distinguished her MAJESTY throughout her long life, were the object of universal esteem and admiration, amongst all classes of his MAJESTY's subjects, and render the death of this Illustrious and most excellent Princess an unspeakable loss to the whole nation.[26]

At 1.00 pm on 17 November 1818, Queen Charlotte closed her eyes for the last time. She expired, Princess Mary recalled, 'without a pang, and [with] a sweet smile on her face.'

Afterword

> The Queen is my physician, and no man need have a
> better; she is my friend, and no man can have a better.

George III's heartfelt words of love for the queen who had been his
champion echoed through the decades of her long and tumultuous
life. The king had no understanding that his wife was dead and,
when her funeral procession made its way to Windsor, straw was
scattered in the courtyard to muffle the sounds of the horses and
the hearse they pulled.

Queen Charlotte lay in state at Kew before making the journey
she had longed for in life. Her mile-long cortege arrived at Windsor
after nightfall on 2 December, pausing at Frogmore before it began
its final journey towards St George's Chapel. The Royal Standard
fluttered at half-mast and the flames of innumerable torches lit
the way to her final resting place. The heartbroken Prince Regent
watched as his mother's ornate coffin was lowered into the vault,
the first consort to enjoy such an honour in almost three centuries.
Fifteen months later, King George III died at Windsor. The loving
husband and wife were reunited in eternal rest.

> I have so many things I could say, but prudence
> imposes silence, and that little dear word silence has
> so often stood my friend in necessity, that I make it
> my constant companion.
>
> Queen Charlotte, 1798

Bibliography

In addition to referenced works:

Anonymous. *Court Life Below Stairs, Vol IV*. London: Hurst and Blackett, 1883.

Anonymous. *George III: His Court and Family, Vol I*. London: Henry Colburn and Co, 1820.

Anonymous. *An Historical Account of the Life and Reign of King George the Fourth*. London: G. Smeeton, 1830.

Aspinall, Arthur (ed.). *The Correspondence of George, Prince of Wales: Vol III*. London: Cassell, 1965.

Aspinall, Arthur (ed.). *The Correspondence of George, Prince of Wales: Vol IV*. London: Cassell, 1965.

Aspinall, Arthur (ed.). *The Correspondence of George, Prince of Wales, Volume VI*. Oxford: Oxford University Press, 1971.

Aspinall, Arthur (ed.). *The Later Correspondence of George III, Vol II*. Cambridge: Cambridge University Press, 1962.

Aspinall, Arthur (ed.). *The Later Correspondence of George III, Vol III*. Cambridge: Cambridge University Press, 1967.

Aspinall, Arthur (ed.). *The Later Correspondence of George III, Vol IV*. Cambridge: Cambridge University Press, 1968.

Aspinall, Arthur (ed.). *The Later Correspondence of George III, Vol V*. Cambridge: Cambridge University Press, 1970.

Aspinall, Arthur (ed.). *Letters of the Princess Charlotte, 1811–1817*. London: Home and Van Thal, 1949.

Baudino, Isabelle & Carré, Jacques. *The Invisible Woman*. London: Routledge, 2017.

Beatty, Michael A. *The English Royal Family of America, from Jamestown to the American Revolution*. Jefferson: McFarland & Company, Inc., 2003.

Belsham, William. *Memoirs of the Reign of George III to the Session of Parliament Ending AD 1793, Vol III*. London: G. G. and J. Robinson, 1801.

Black, Jeremy. *George III: America's Last King*. New Haven: Yale University Press, 2008.

Black, Jeremy. *The Hanoverians: The History of a Dynasty*. London: Hambledon and London, 2007.

Buckingham and Chandos, Duke of. *Memoirs of the Court of George IV, Vol I*. London: Hurst and Blackett, 1859.

Burney, Frances. *The Diary and Letters of Frances Burney, Madame D'Arblay, Vol I*. Boston: Little, Brown and Company, 1910.

Burney, Frances. *Diary and Letters of Madame D'Arblay, Vol VI*. London: Henry Colburn, 1854.

Bury, Lady Charlotte Campbell. *Diary Illustrative of the Times of George the Fourth: Vol II*. London: Carey, Lea and Blanchard, 1838.

Bury, Lady Charlotte Campbell. *Diary Illustrative of the Times of George the Fourth: Vol III*. London: Henry Colburn, 1839.

Campbell Orr, Clarissa. *Queenship in Europe 1660–1815: The Role of the Consort*. Cambridge: Cambridge University Press, 2004.

Catania, Steven, 'Brandy Nan and Farmer George: Public Perceptions of Royal Health and the Demystification of English Monarchy During the Long Eighteenth Century' (2014). Dissertations. Paper 1255. http://ecommons.luc.edu/luc_diss/1255.

Chapman, Hester W. *Caroline Matilda, Queen of Denmark, 1751–75*. London: Cape, 1971.

Clarke, ML, 'The Education of Royalty in the Eighteenth Century: George IV and William IV.' *British Journal of Educational*

Studies, vol. 26, no. 1, 1978, pp. 73–87. JSTOR, www.jstor.org/stable/3120477.

Coulton, WC. *Authentic and Impartial Memoirs of Her Late Majesty, Charlotte, Queen of Great Britain and Ireland.* London: T. Kinnersley, 1819.

Craig, William Marshall. *Memoir of Her Majesty Sophia Charlotte of Mecklenburg Strelitz, Queen of Great Britain.* Liverpool: Henry Fisher, 1818.

Curtis, Edith Roelker. *Lady Sarah Lennox, An Irrepressible Stuart.* New York: G. P. Putnam's Sons, 1946.

Curzon, Catherine. *The Daughters of George III: Sisters & Princesses.* Barnsley: Pen & Sword, 2020.

Curzon, Catherine. *The Elder Sons of George III: Kings, Princes & a Grand Old Duke.* Barnsley: Pen & Sword, 2020.

Curzon, Catherine. *Kings of Georgian Britain.* Barnsley: Pen & Sword, 2017.

Curzon, Catherine. *Queens of Georgian Britain.* Barnsley: Pen & Sword, 2017.

David, Saul. *Prince of Pleasure.* New York: Grove Press, 2000.

Delves Broughton, Vernon (ed.). *Court and Private Life in the Time of Queen Charlotte.* London: Richard Bentley, 1887.

Dickenson, Mary Hamilton. *Mary Hamilton: Afterwards Mrs. John Dickenson, at Court and at Home.* London: John Murray, 1925.

Donne, Bodham W. (ed.). *The Correspondence of King George the Third With Lord North from 1768 to 1783: Vol I.* London: John Murray, 1867.

Doran, John. *Lives of the Queens of England of the House of Hanover, Volume I.* New York: Redfield, 1855.

Doran, John. *Lives of the Queens of England of the House of Hanover, Volume II.* Boston, Francis A. Niccolls & Co, 1900.

Fitzgerald, Percy. *The Good Queen Charlotte.* London: Downey & Co, 1899.

Fitzgerald, Percy. *The Life and Times of William IV, Vol I*. London: Tinsley Brothers, 1884.

Fitzgerald, Percy. *The Life and Times of William IV, Vol II*. London: Tinsley Brothers, 1884.

Fitzgerald, Percy. *The Life of George the Fourth*. London: Tinsley Brothers, 1881.

Fitzgerald, Percy. *The Royal Dukes and Princesses of the Family of George III, Vol I*. London: Tinsley Brothers, 1882.

Fitzgerald, Percy. *The Royal Dukes and Princesses of the Family of George III, Vol II*. London: Tinsley Brothers, 1882.

Fraser, Flora. *The Unruly Queen: The Life of Queen Caroline*. Edinburgh: A&C Black, 2012.

Gilmour, Ian. *Riot, Risings and Revolution: Governance and Violence in Eighteenth-Century England*. London: Pimlico, 1993.

Glenbervie, Sylvester Douglas. *The Diaries of Sylvester Douglas, Lord Glenbervie*. London: Constable & Co Ltd., 1928.

Hadlow, Janice. *The Strangest Family: The Private Lives of George III, Queen Charlotte and the Hanoverians*. London: William Collins, 2014.

Hall, Matthew. *The Royal Princesses of England*. London: George Routledge and Sons, 1871.

Harris, George. *The Life of Lord Chancellor Hardwicke, Vol III*. London: Edward Moxon, 1847.

Hibbert, Christopher. *George III: A Personal History*. London: Viking, 1998.

Hibbert, Christopher. *George IV*. London: Penguin, 1998.

Hill, Constance. *Fanny Burney at the Court of Queen Charlotte*. London: John Lane, 1912.

Holt, Edward. *The Public and Domestic Life of His Late Most Gracious Majesty, George the Third, Vol I*. London: Sherwood, Neely and Jones, 1820.

Holt, Edward. *The Public and Domestic Life of His Late Most Gracious Majesty, George the Third, Vol II*. London: Sherwood, Neely and Jones, 1820.

Huish, Robert. *Memoirs of George the Fourth, Vol I*. London: Thomas Kelly, 1830.

Huish, Robert. *Memoirs of Her Late Majesty Caroline, Queen of Great Britain*. London: Thomas Kelly, 1821.

Huish, Robert. *The Public and Private Life of His Late Excellent and Most Gracious Majesty, George the Third*. London: Thomas Kelly, 1821.

Hunt, Margaret. *Women in Eighteenth-Century Europe*. New York: Routledge, 2010.

Ilchester, Countess of & Stavordale, Lord (eds.). *The Life and Letters of Lady Sarah Lennox*. London: John Murray, 1902.

Irvine, Valerie. *The King's Wife: George IV and Mrs Fitzherbert*. London: Hambledon, 2007.

Jesse, John Heneage. *Memoirs of the Life and Reign of King George the Third, Vol II*. London: Tinsley Brothers, 1867.

Jesse, John Heneage. *Memoirs of the Life and Reign of King George the Third, Vol III*. London: Richard Bentley, 1843.

Jesse, John Heneage. *Memoirs of the Life and Reign of King George the Third, Vol IV*. Boston: L. C. Page & Company, 1902.

Lancelott, Francis. *The Queens of England and Their Times: Volume II*. New York: D. Appleton and Co., 1859.

Lehman, H. Eugene. *Lives of England's Reigning and Consort Queens*. Bloomington: AuthorHouse, 2011.

Leslie, Anita. *Mrs Fitzherbert: A Biography*. York: Scribner, 1960.

Leslie, Shane. *Mrs. Fitzherbert: A Life Chiefly from Unpublished Sources*. New York: Benziger Brothers, 1939.

Llanover, Lady. *The Autobiography and Correspondence of Mary Granville, Mrs Delany, Vol II*. London: Richard Bentley, 1862.

Llanover, Lady. *The Autobiography and Correspondence of Mary Granville, Mrs Delany, Vol III*. London: Richard Bentley, 1862.

Lovat-Fraser, J. A. *John Stuart Earl of Bute*. Cambridge: Cambridge University Press, 1912.

Melville, Lewis. *Farmer George, Vol I*. London: Sir Isaac Pitman and Sons, Ltd, 1907.

Oulton, C. W. *Authentic and Impartial Memoirs of Her Late Majesty: Charlotte Queen of Great Britain and Ireland*. London: J. Robins and Co., 1818.

Papendiek, Charlotte. *Court and Private Life in the Time of Queen Charlotte, Vol II*. London: Richard Bentley & Son, 1887.

Peters, T. J. & Beveridge, A. 'The Blindness, Deafness and Madness of King George III: Psychiatric Interactions' (2010). *The Journal of the Royal College of Physicians of Edinburgh*, Vol. 40, Issue 1. www.rcpe.ac.uk/sites/default/files/peters_1.pdf.

Robins, Jane. *The Trial of Queen Caroline*: *The Scandalous Affair that Nearly Ended a Monarchy*. New York: Simon and Schuster, 2006.

Roelker Curtis, Edith. *Lady Sarah Lennox: An Irrepressible Stuart*. New York: G. P. Putnam's Sons, 1946.

Sanders, Margaret. *Intimate Letters of England's Queens*. Stroud: Amberley, 2014.

Sedgwick, Romney (ed.). *Letters from George III to Lord Bute 1756–1766*. London: Macmillan and Co. Ltd., 1939.

Seeley, L. A. (ed.). *Fanny Burney (Madame D'Arblay) and Her Friends*. New York: Scribner and Welford, 1890.

Smith, E. A. *George IV*. New Haven: Yale University Press, 1999.

Spencer, Sarah. *Correspondence of Sarah Spencer Lady Lyttelton 1787–1870*. London: John Murray, 1912.

Tidridge, Nathan. *Prince Edward, Duke of Kent*. Dundurn: Toronto, 2013.

Tillyard, Stella. *A Royal Affair: George III and his Troublesome Siblings*. London: Vintage, 2007.

Toynbee, Paget (ed.). *The Letters of Horace Walpole, Vol VI*. Oxford: Clarendon Press, 1904.

Toynbee, Paget (ed.). *The Letters of Horace Walpole, Vol XI.* Oxford: Clarendon Press, 1904.

Toynbee, Paget (ed.). *The Letters of Horace Walpole, Vol XIII.* Oxford: Clarendon Press, 1905.

Toynbee, Paget (ed.). *The Letters of Horace Walpole, Vol XV.* Oxford: Clarendon Press, 1905.

Toynbee, Paget (ed.). *Supplement to the Letters of Horace Walpole, Vol III.* Oxford: Clarendon Press, 1905.

Toynbee, Paget (ed.). *Supplement to the Letters of Horace Walpole, Vol VII.* Oxford: Clarendon Press, 1905.

Walpole, Horace. *Letters of Horace Walpole, Earl of Orford, to Sir Horace Mann.* London: Richard Bentley, 1833.

Walpole, Horace. *Letters of Horace Walpole, Earl of Orford, to Sir Horace Mann, Vol II.* Philadelphia: Lea & Blanchard, 1844.

Walpole, Horace. *Letters of Horace Walpole, Earl of Orford, to Sir Horace Mann, Vol III.* London: Richard Bentley, 1833.

Walpole, Horace. *Letters of Horace Walpole, Earl of Orford, to Sir Horace Mann, Vol IV.* London: Richard Bentley, 1844.

Walpole, Horace. *The Letters of Horace Walpole: Vol I.* London: Lea and Blanchard, 1842.

Walpole, Horace. *The Letters of Horace Walpole: Vol II.* New York: Dearborn, 1832.

Walpole, Horace. *Memoirs of the Reign of King George the Third: Vol II.* Philadelphia: Lea & Blanchard, 1845.

Walpole, Horace. *Memoirs of the Reign of King George the Third: Vol III.* London: Richard Bentley, 1845.

Walpole, Horace. *Memoirs of the Reign of King George the Third: Vol IV.* London: Richard Bentley, 1845.

Walpole, Horace and Doran, John (ed.). *Journal of the Reign of King George the Third, Vol I.* London, Richard Bentley, 1859.

Walpole, Horace and Doran, John (ed.). *Journal of the Reign of King George the Third, Vol II.* London, Richard Bentley, 1859.

Walpole, Horace. *The Last Journals of Horace Walpole During the Reign of George III from 1771–1783*. London: John Lane, 1910.

Watkins, John. *Memoirs of Her Most Excellent Majesty Sophia Charlotte, Queen of Great Britain*. London: Henry Colburn, 1819.

Williams, Thomas. *Memoirs of Her Late Majesty Queen Charlotte*. London: W. Simpkin and R. Marshall, 1819.

Williams, Thomas. *Memoirs of His Late Majesty George III*. London: W. Simpkin and R. Marshall, 1820.

Woolsey, Sarah Chauncey. *The Diary and Letters of Frances Burney, Madame D'Arblay, Vol I*. Boston: Little, Brown, and Company, 1910.

Newspapers

All newspaper clippings are reproduced © The British Library Board; in addition to those cited, innumerable newspapers were consulted.

Websites Consulted

British History Online (www.british-history.ac.uk)

British Library Newspapers (www.gale.com/intl/primary-sources/british-library-newspapers)

Georgian Papers Online (https://gpp.royalcollection.org.uk)

Hansard (http://hansard.millbanksystems.com/index.html)

Historical Texts (http://historicaltexts.jisc.ac.uk)

House of Commons Parliamentary Papers (http://parlipapers.chadwyck.co.uk/marketing/index.jsp)

JSTOR (www.jstor.org)

The National Archives (www.nationalarchives.gov.uk)

Oxford Dictionary of National Biography (www.oxforddnb.com)
Queen Victoria's Journals (www.queenvictoriasjournals.org)
State Papers Online (www.gale.com/intl/primary-sources/
  statepapers-online)
The Times Archive (www.thetimes.co.uk/archive)

Notes

The Royal Family

1. Toynbee, Paget (ed.) (1904). *The Letters of Horace Walpole, Vol VIII*. Oxford: Clarendon Press, p. 381.

Introduction

1. Walpole, Horace (1843). *Letters of Horace Walpole, Earl of Orford, to Sir Horace Mann, Vol I*. London: Richard Bentley, p. 41.

Act One: Princess

1. Carlyle, Thomas (1866). *History of Friedrich the Second, Called Frederick the Great, Vol II*. New York: Harper & Brothers, p. 478.
2. In addition to the marriage of Charlotte and George III, Charlotte's niece, Princess Louise, married Frederick William III to become Queen Consort of Prussia. A second niece, Princess Frederica, married Charlotte's son, Ernest Augustus, Duke of Cumberland and Teviotdale, and became Queen Consort of Hanover.
3. Elisabeth Albertine briefly ruled as Regent until her son reached the age of majority. Whilst doing so, she successfully defended the family duchies against encroachments from Duke Christian Ludwig II of Mecklenburg-Schwerin.

4. Deluc became reader to Queen Charlotte in 1773 and retained the role for forty-four years. Whilst in Charlotte's employ, she was his patron when he undertook geological tours around Europe. Today, Deluc's name is honoured as one of the craters on the moon.

5. Charlotte's daughter, the Princess Royal, would later become the first Queen of Württemberg.

6. Nugent, Thomas (1768). *Travels Through Germany, Vol I.* London: Edward and Charles Dilly, pp. 243–344.

7. A fire had ravaged Strelitz in 1712 and the ducal court relocated to a hunting lodge named *Zierker See*. The town of Neustrelitz was constructed around the lodge.

8. He later reigned as Charles II, Grand Duke of Mecklenburg.

9. Clark, J. C. D. (ed.) (1988). *The Memoirs and Speeches of James, 2nd Earl Waldegrave, 1742–1763.* Cambridge: Cambridge University Press, p. 165.

10. Waldegrave, James (1821). *Memoirs from 1754 to 1758.* London: John Murray, p. 41.

11. Namier, L. B. (ed.) (1939). *Letters from George III to Lord Bute, 1756–1766.* London: MacMillan and Co Ltd, p. 37.

12. Walpole, Horace (1845). *Memoirs of the Reign of King George the Third: Vol I.* Philadelphia: Lea & Blanchard, p. 47.

13. Namier, L. B. (ed.) (1939). *Letters from George III to Lord Bute, 1756–1766.* London: MacMillan and Co Ltd, p. 40.

14. *Whitehall Evening Post or London Intelligencer*, 23–25 October 1760; issue 2,279.

15. Walpole, Horace (1845). *Memoirs of the Reign of King George the Third, Vol I.* Philadelphia: Lea & Blanchard, p. 63.

16. Ibid.

17. Namier, L. B. (ed.) (1939). *Letters from George III to Lord Bute, 1756–1766.* London: MacMillan and Co Ltd, p. 40.

18. Lady Sarah's eventual marriage to Sir Charles Bunbury, 6th Baronet, was plagued by scandal and ended when she eloped

with Lord William Gordon and bore him a child. Though her first marriage ended in divorce, Lady Sarah's second marriage, to the Honourable George Napier, was a very happy one indeed.

19. Quennell, Peter (ed.) (1960). *History Today*. London: Bracken House, p. 374.

20. Walpole, Horace (1843). *Letters of Horace Walpole, Earl of Orford, to Sir Horace Mann, Vol I*. London: Richard Bentley, p. 9.

21. Barrett, Charlotte (ed.) (1876). *Diary and Letters of Madame D'Arblay, Vol II*. London, Chatto and Windus, p. 51.

22. Namier, L. B. (ed.) (1939). *Letters from George III to Lord Bute, 1756–1766*. London: MacMillan and Co Ltd, p. 53.

23. Ibid., p. 54.

24. Ibid., p. 55.

25. Ibid., p. 53.

26. Ibid., p. 55.

27. Ibid., p. 56.

28. Ibid., p. 57.

29. Ibid., p. 57.

30. Ibid., p. 58.

31. *London Gazette Extraordinary*, 8 July 1761.

32. Walpole, Horace (1843). *Letters of Horace Walpole, Earl of Orford, to Sir Horace Mann, Vol I*. London: Richard Bentley, pp. 32–33.

33. 'Come, don't be childish – you are to be Queen of England.'

34. Jesse, John Heneage (1867). *Memoirs of the Life and Reign of King George the Third, Vol I*. London: Tinsley Brothers, p. 92.

35. Namier, L. B. (ed.) (1939). *Letters from George III to Lord Bute, 1756–1766*. London: MacMillan and Co Ltd, p. 61.

36. Anonymous (1813). *The Parliamentary History of England, from the Earliest Period to the Year 1803, Vol XV*. London: Longman, Hurst, Rees, Orme, & Brown, p. 1110.

37. Jesse, John Heneage (1867). *Memoirs of the Life and Reign of King George the Third, Vol I.* London: Tinsley Brothers, p. 94.

38. *Public Advertiser*, 8 August 1761; issue 8,350.

39. Papendiek was in no hurry to leave his homeland but Charlotte insisted, even contriving to ensure he had married before his departure in order to avoid any whisper of scandal. His new bride was left behind for two years, until friends paid her passage to England.

40. *Lloyd's Evening Post*, 21–24 August 1761; issue 641.

41. Anonymous (ed.) (1761). *The Scots Magazine, Vol XXIII.* Edinburgh: W. Sands, A. Murray and J. Cochran, p. 491.

42. *Lloyd's Evening Post*, 2–4 September 1761; issue 646.

43. Namier, L. B. (ed.) (1939). *Letters from George III to Lord Bute, 1756–1766.* London: MacMillan and Co Ltd, p. 62.

44. *St James's Chronicle, or the British Evening Post.* 8 September 1761; issue 78.

45. Anonymous (1813). *The Parliamentary History of England, from the Earliest Period to the Year 1803, Vol XV.* London: Longman, Hurst, Rees, Orme, & Brown, p. 1111.

46. Fitzgerald, Emilia Mary Lennox, Duchess of Leinster (1949). *Letters of Emily, Duchess of Leinster, James, First Duke of Leinster, Caroline Fox, Lady Holland, Vol I.* London: Stationery Office, p. 113.

47. Ribeiro, Aileen (1984). *Dress in Eighteenth-Century Europe.* London: BT Batsford, p. 135.

48. Papendiek, Charlotte (1887). *Mrs Papendiek's Journals, Vol I.* London: Richard Bentley & Son, p. 12.

49. Walpole, Horace (1843). *Letters of Horace Walpole, Earl of Orford, to Sir Horace Mann, Vol I.* London: Richard Bentley, p. 41.

50. *London Evening Post*, 8–10 September 1761; issue 5,283.

51. Montagu, Matthew (ed.) (1813). *The Letters of Mrs Elizabeth Montagu, Part the Second, Vol IV.* London: T. Cadell and W. Davies, p. 368.

52. Anonymous (1871). *Miscellanies of the Philobiblon Society, Vol XIII.* London: The Philobiblon Society, p. 44.

53. Later, the provision of Somerset House was exchanged for Buckingham House.

54. Howard, Jean, Sinfield, Alan, and Smith, Lindsay (2005). *Luxurious Sexualities: Textual Practice*, Volume 11, issue 3. London: Routledge, p. 65.

55. Toynbee, Paget (ed.) (1904). *The Letters of Horace Walpole, Vol VII.* Oxford: Clarendon Press, p. 7.

56. Toynbee, Paget (ed.) (1904). *The Letters of Horace Walpole, Vol VI.* Oxford: Clarendon Press, p. 99.

57. Anonymous (1871). *Miscellanies of the Philobiblon Society, Vol XIII.* London: The Philobiblon Society, p. 45.

58. Greenwood, Alice Drayton (1911). *Lives of the Hanoverian Queens of England, Vol II.* London: Chiswick Press, p. 222.

59. Toynbee, Paget (ed.) (1904). *The Letters of Horace Walpole, Vol IX.* Oxford: Clarendon Press, p. 147.

60. Aspinall, Arthur (ed.) (1962). *The Later Correspondence of George III: Vol I.* Cambridge: Cambridge University Press, p. 234.

Act Two: Queen

1. Stanhope, Philip Dormer, 4th Earl of Chesterfield (1838). *The Works of Lord Chesterfield.* New York: Harper & Brothers, p. 588.

2. Hunter served as Physician Extraordinary to the Queen.

3. *Gazetteer and London Daily Advertiser*, 13 August 1762; issue 10,392.

4. Namier, L. B. (ed.) (1939). *Letters from George III to Lord Bute, 1756–1766.* London: MacMillan and Co Ltd, p. 134.

5. Born in 1763 and 1765 respectively. William would reign as William IV.

6. Georgian Papers Online (http://gpp.rct.uk, February 2021; hereafter referred to as GPP) RA GEO/ADD/15/8157: Queen Charlotte to Lady Charlotte Finch, 7 October 1775.

7. GPP, RA GEO/ADD/10/1: Princess Augusta to Queen Charlotte, 26 December 1777.

8. *Whitehall Evening Post or London Intelligencer*, 26–28 October 1769; issue 3,677.

9. GPP, RA GEO/MAIN/36345-36347: Queen Charlotte to George, Prince of Wales, 12 August 1770.

10. GPP, RA GEO/ADD/4/204/9: Queen Charlotte to Prince William, 28 July 1780.

11. Craik, George Lillie & MacFarlane, Charles (1814) (ed.). *The Pictorial History of England During the Reign of King George the Third, Vol I*. London: Charles Knight and Co, p. 126.

12. GPP, RA GEO/ADD/15/8154: Queen Charlotte to Lady Charlotte Finch, 1774–1775.

13. Ibid.

14. *Middlesex Journal or Chronicle of Liberty*, 8–11 February 1772; issue 447.

15. The queen's actual birthday was on 19 May, just a fortnight before that of her husband. Due to this proximity, it was decided that she would celebrate her official birthday in January instead.

16. Walpole, Horace (1910). *The Last Journals of Horace Walpole During the Reign of George III from 1771–1783*. London: John Lane, p. 17.

17. GPP, RA GEO/MAIN/43469-43471: George, Prince of Wales to Prince Frederick, 22 October 1781.

18. GPP, RA GEO/ADD/4/204/26: Queen Charlotte to Prince William, 30 December 1782.

19. The Queen's Lodge was demolished by George IV in 1823, in order to improve his view of the Long Walk.

20. GPP, RA GEO/ADD/15/8160: Queen Charlotte to Lady Charlotte Finch, 6 June 1782.

21. GPP, RA GEO/ADD/15/443a-b: Queen Charlotte to Lady Charlotte Finch, August 1782.

22. GPP, RA GEO/ADD/4/17: Queen Charlotte to Prince William, 4 September 1782.

23. Ibid.

24. Burney, Frances (1910). *The Diary and Letters of Frances Burney, Madame D'Arblay, Vol II*. Boston: Little, Brown and Company, p. 27.

25. Burney, Frances (1842). *Diary and Letters of Madame D'Arblay, Vol IV*. London: Henry Colburn, p. 285.

26. Ibid., pp. 287–288.

27. Ibid., p. 288.

28. Burney, Frances (1842). *Diary and Letters of Madame D'Arblay, Vol III*. London: Henry Colburn, p. 171.

29. *The Times*, 26 December 1788; issue 1,215.

30. Minto, Emma Eleanor Elizabeth (ed.) (1874). *Life and Letters of Sir Gilbert Elliot, First Earl of Minto, from 1751 to 1806, Vol I*. London: Longmans, p. 292.

31. Berkeley, Helen (ed.) (1844). *Memoirs of Madame d'Arblay, Vol I*. London: James Mowatt & Co, p. 23.

32. Ibid.

33. Ibid.

34. *The Times*, 11 December 1788; issue 1,203.

35. Aspinall, Arthur (ed.) (1965). *The Correspondence of George, Prince of Wales: Vol I*. London: Cassell, p. 405.

36. Toynbee, Paget (ed.) (1905). *The Letters of Horace Walpole, Vol XIV*. Oxford: Clarendon Press, p. 112.

37. GPP, RA GEO/MAIN/38429-38433: Prince of Wales to Queen Charlotte, 30 January 1789.

38. GPP, RA GEO/MAIN/36377-36378: Queen Charlotte to the Prince of Wales, 1 February 1789.

39. Woolsey, Sarah Chauncey (1910). *The Diary and Letters of Frances Burney, Madame D'Arblay, Vol II*. Boston: Roberts Brothers, p. 126.

40. GPP, RCIN 1047014 Journal of Robert Fulke Greville, Volume 2, October 1788–4 March 1789.

41. Minto, Emma Eleanor Elizabeth (ed.) (1874). *Life and Letters of Sir Gilbert Elliot, First Earl of Minto, from 1751 to 1806, Vol I*. London: Longmans, p. 287.

42. GPP, RA GEO/MAIN/16366: George III to Colonel George Hotham, 21 June 1783.

43. GPP, RA GEO/MAIN/36395-8: Queen Charlotte to the Prince of Wales, 2 September 1792.

44. Aspinall, Arthur (ed.) (1962). *The Later Correspondence of George III, Vol I*. Cambridge: Cambridge University Press, p. 525.

45. Levey, Michael (2005). *Sir Thomas Lawrence*. New Haven: Yale University Press, p. 20.

46. Aspinall, Arthur (ed.) (1965). *The Correspondence of George, Prince of Wales: Vol. III*. London: Cassell, p. 9.

47. GPP, RA GEO/MAIN/36479: Queen Charlotte to the Prince of Wales, 14 December 1796.

48. Anson, Sir Archibald Edward Harbord (1920). *About Others and Myself, 1745–1920*. London: John Murray, p. 17.

49. Aspinall, Arthur (ed.) (1963). *The Correspondence of George, Prince of Wales: Vol II*. London: Cassell, p. 388.

50. Aspinall, Arthur (ed.) (1920). *Later Correspondence of George III: December 1783 to January 1793*. Cambridge: Cambridge University Press, p. 14.

51. GPP, RA GEO/MAIN/49204: Prince of Wales to the Countess of Elgin, 20 August 1797.

52. For his work with George III, Willis received a pension of £1,500 a year for the rest of his life. His son, Dr John Willis, received an annuity of £650 a year for life. Willis further

enhanced his reputation and his personal fortune after being paid £16,000 to treat the madness of Queen Maria I of Portugal, though he eventually declared her incurable. As a result of their fame, the Willises' private sanatorium at Greatford Hall in Lincolnshire became so popular that they had to open a second at Shillingthorpe Hall. Dr Francis Willis died in 1807.

53. GPP, RA GEO/ADD/12/1/28: Princess Mary to the Prince of Wales, 13 February 1804.

54. Aspinall, Arthur (ed.) (1965). *The Correspondence of George, Prince of Wales: Vol V*. London: Cassell, p. 90.

55. Ibid., p. 114.

56. Harcourt, Leveson Vernon (ed.) (1860). *The Diaries and Correspondence of the Right Hon. George Rose, Vol II*. London: Richard Bentley, pp. 193–194.

57. Winslow, Forbes (ed.) (1857). *The Journal of Psychological Medicine and Mental Pathology, Vol X*. London: John Churchill, p. 114.

58. I tell their stories in *The Daughters of George III: Sisters & Princesses* (Pen & Sword, 2020).

59. GPP, RA GEO/MAIN/36545-36546: Queen Charlotte to George III, 7 April 1805.

60. Iremonger, Lucille (1958). *Love and the Princesses*. New York: Thomas Y. Crowell Company, p. 146.

61. Malmesbury, 3rd Earl of (ed.) (1844). *Diaries and Correspondence of James Harris, First Earl of Malmesbury, Vol III*. London: Richard Bentley, p. 154.

Act Three: Guardian

1. Murray, The Honourable Amelia (1868). *Recollections from 1803 to 1837*. London: Longmans, Green, and Co., pp. 25–26.

2. GPP, RA GEO/ADD/2/92: Queen Charlotte to George III, 22 April 1810.

3. *Hampshire Telegraph and Sussex Chronicle etc.*, 5 November 1810; issue 578.

4. FitzRoy married Eliza Barlow in 1816. Thanks to his discretion, he remained in royal favour. Following his death in 1831, his wife confirmed that she believed her husband and Amelia had been married, but no evidence exists to prove it.

5. *The Times*, 21 December 1810; issue 8,171.

6. GPP, RA GEO/MAIN/36583-36586: Queen Charlotte to the Prince Regent, 10 November 1811.

7. Flower, B (1811). *Flower's Political Review and Monthly Miscellany, Vol IX.* Harlow: B Flower, p. 54.

8 Perceval's career was eventually ended by an assassin the following year. To date, he is the only British prime minister to have been the victim of an assassination.

9. Flower, B (1811). *Flower's Political Review and Monthly Miscellany, Vol IX.* Harlow: B Flower, p. 11.

10. GPP, RA GEO/MAIN/36566: Queen Charlotte to the Prince Regent, 8 February 1811.

11. GPP, RA GEO/ADD/10/52: Queen Charlotte to Princesses Augusta, Elizabeth, Mary and Sophia, 2 April 1812.

12. Ibid.

13. GPP, RA GEO/ADD/10/59: Princess Augusta to the Prince Regent, 23 January 1812.

14. GPP, RA GEO/ADD/10/56: Princess Augusta to the Prince Regent, 5 March 1812.

15. Taylor, Ernest (ed.) (1913). *The Taylor Papers.* London: Longmans, Green, and Co, pp. 78–79.

16. Malmesbury, 3rd Earl of (ed.) (1844). *Diaries and Correspondence of James Harris, First Earl of Malmesbury, Vol III.* London: Richard Bentley, p. 155.

17. Stanhope, Lady Hester (1846). *Memoirs of the Lady Hester Stanhope, Vol I.* London: Henry Colburn, p. 267.

18. GPP, RA GEO/ADD/15/8138: Queen Charlotte to Lord Liverpool, 11 February 1813.
19. GPP, RA GEO/MAIN/36666: Queen Charlotte to the Prince Regent, 14 December 1813.
20. *The Times*, 17 January 1816; issue 9,733.
21. *The Morning Chronicle*, 8 November 1817; issue 15,139.
22. Rush, Richard (1833). *Memoranda of a Residence at the Court of London*. Philadelphia: Carey, Lea & Blanchard, p. 174.
23. Hedley, Olwen (1975). *Queen Charlotte*. London: J. Murray, p.294.
24. *The Times*, 8 September 1818; issue 10,456.
25. *Hampshire Telegraph and Sussex Chronicle etc.*, 16 November 1818; issue 997.
26. *Morning Post*, 18 November 1818; issue 14,923.

Index